TAYLOR
LAUTNER

TAYLOR LAUTNER

A-Z

S A R A H   O L I V E R

JOHN BLAKE

Published by John Blake Publishing Ltd,
3 Bramber Court, 2 Bramber Road,
London W14 9PB, England

www.johnblakepublishing.co.uk

First published in paperback in 2010

ISBN: 978 1 84358 247 2

British Library Cataloguing-in-Publication Data:

A catalogue record for this book is available from the British Library.

Design by www.envydesign.co.uk

Printed in Great Britain by CPI Bookmarque, Croydon, CR0 4TD

3 5 7 9 10 8 6 4 2

All images © Wenn

Papers used by John Blake Publishing are natural, recyclable products made from
wood grown in sustainable forests. The manufacturing processes conform to the
environmental regulations of the country of origin.

All photographs have been supplied courtesy of WENN Images.

Dedicated, with love, to my mum and dad.

Introduction

The *Taylor Lautner A–Z* is jam-packed with everything you need to know about Taylor. No other book goes into so much detail, tells all the set secrets and reveals why Taylor gets on so well with female Taylors.

Sarah Oliver has written over 800 articles on Taylor and all things *Twilight*. She has been fortunate enough to meet him in the flesh and knows more about him than any other journalist on the planet. Her articles on *Twilight* have been viewed by over 10 million people.

Sarah has worked with *Twilight* fans across the world to produce the most up-to-date guide to everyone's favourite werewolf. You can read this book from start to finish, or dip in and out of it, if you prefer.

A is for...

Abduction

Since Taylor proved to the world in *New Moon* that he was a great actor he has been inundated with great movie roles. He is one of the most popular celebrities in the world, so studios are desperate to snap him up for their latest projects.

In 2011 we will get to see Taylor in a new thriller called *Abduction*, directed by John Singleton. He will be playing the lead – a young man called Nathan, who finds his own baby photo on a missing persons website. Nathan has always had a strained relationship with his parents but once he finds out the truth, he is put in tremendous danger and has to run for his life. *Abduction* was filmed during July 2010 in Pittsburgh.

At least one scene in this movie will involve Taylor taking off his top as his love interest carefully removes shards of glass from his chest after he is nearly killed in an explosion. It sounds full of exciting action like the Jason Bourne stories so there may be more films to follow.

This is going to be a massive movie as John Singleton is a superb director. He directed Mark Wahlberg in *Four Brothers*, Samuel L. Jackson and Tom Cruise in *Shaft* and Paul Walker in *2 Fast 2 Furious*. Taylor could easily end up being nominated for an Oscar if he puts in a good performance.

Acting

Most young actors start out acting in their school plays and decide to become professional because they are passionate about acting and love being on the stage or in front of a camera. Some young actors like *Harry Potter* star Daniel Radcliffe have parents who are involved in the movie business – his mum was a casting agent and his dad was a literary agent. Other big names like Angelina Jolie, Ben Stiller and Kate Hudson all have parents who are actors, so they already have acting in their blood.

TAYLOR WITH HIS *TWILIGHT* CO-STARS, KRISTEN STEWART AND ROBERT PATTINSON.

Taylor Lautner doesn't have a typical acting background at all – his parents had nothing to do with the acting world and he wasn't discovered when performing in a play, like his *Twilight* co-stars Robert Pattinson and Kristen Stewart. Taylor's fans instead have his martial arts instructor, Mike Chat, to thank for suggesting that he should give acting a try.

Taylor explained to *The Grand Rapids Press* why Mike singled him out for movie work: 'He saw that I wasn't shy, that I was confident, that I talked a lot.' He also happened to be a very cute kid and his teacher must have known that his looks would appeal to casting directors and fans alike.

Lots of martial arts experts have made the move into acting – Mike Chat himself played a Power Ranger. Also, there's Bruce Lee and Jean-Claude Van Damme. Taylor is just the latest in a long line.

Despite being so talented as an actor and performer, Taylor has had to deal with rejection and not getting parts from a young age and so he wants to encourage budding actors to keep going. He told UltimateDisney.com, 'My advice for people that want to act would definitely be: "You can't get down." Because the average booking rate when you're starting is one out of 75 auditions and that's crazy! So you can't just go to something and not get it, and get totally down and want to quit, because that's just not happening unless you're an extremely lucky and talented person. But once you break into the business more, it will get better. You just can't get down and quit because it's very, very difficult.'

To improve his acting skills Taylor signed up for classes to make sure that he would perform well in auditions. He also wanted to improve his other skills, so he took dance classes and got a voice coach too. Taylor was prepared to do whatever it took to succeed and sacrificed a lot of his own free time to learn how to be a better actor.

Ads

Taylor has always been good-looking and so he appeared in advertisements as well as acting when he was younger. He once did an advert for *Frosted Flakes*, which was a big hit – Taylor played a baseball player for the 'Tigers' and had to show off his baseball and running skills. He became the leader of the team when they were filming and got the other boys to chant the lines that the director wanted them to say. At the end of the television ad, all the boys are sitting round a big table eating *Frosted Flakes* but the camera focuses on Taylor as he eats and then smiles next to the cereal box.

Taylor's family was very proud when Taylor landed

A 13-YEAR-OLD TAYLOR SMILES FOR THE CAMERA.

this part, even though it was just a TV ad. They went along and filmed a home movie of Taylor behind the scenes. Taylor did really well as it took quite a while to film the ad and he had to keep having his make-up reapplied because of the glare of the lights overhead. He also had to eat lots of cereal as they reshot the scenes several times!

Anna Kendrick

Anna Kendrick plays Jessica in the *Twilight Saga* movies and is one of Taylor's friends. Like Taylor, Anna was a child actor first and so she had a lot of audition experience when she attended the *Twilight* casting. Anna really wanted to be in *Twilight* as she loved the story.

Poor Anna didn't have a great first audition for *Twilight* – she wasn't feeling at all well, so had to leave before it finished. Thankfully she was invited back and got to audition again. That time around, she impressed everyone with her acting skills and soon got the news that she would be playing the part of Jessica.

The Jessica we see in the *Twilight* movies is different from the character that *Twilight* author Stephenie Meyer created because the *Twilight* screenwriter Melissa Rosenberg decided to combine Lauren Mallory and Jessica Stanley to make one character.

ANNA KENDRICK IS ONE OF TAYLOR'S CLOSEST FRIENDS.

Taylor has many friends on the *Twilight* cast and Anna is just one of them. She thinks he is really special and enjoys hanging out with him when they're not filming. Shortly before *New Moon* came out, Anna told E! Online that she thought the new Jacob we see in the movie would cause some Edward fans to swap sides and join 'Team Jacob': 'Taylor will certainly capture the hearts of many people who thought they only had eyes for Rob – he's so cute, he's such a cutie.'

She has also said in the past: 'You meet Taylor and there's something really special about him, he's so warm. He's so different from Rob and different from Kristen. There's something about him that feels he's sort of built for this.'

Sometimes it might seem as if Anna could have a bit of a crush on Taylor because of the nice things she says about him in interviews but that isn't the case. They are just good friends and in many ways have a sister/brother type of relationship. After all, Anna is six years older than our favourite actor.

Anna might be popular but her fan base is a lot smaller than Taylor's. In fact, her most memorable encounter was meeting one of Taylor's fans, not one of her own fans. She explained what happened to *Entertainment Weekly*: 'There was a girl in Vancouver, who came up to me in a store and asked me to give something to Taylor the next time that I saw him, and I just said I wasn't sure the next time

I would see him, so I didn't want to take it because I didn't really know when it was going to be. She said it as though she had it with her, as if she carried it around just in case she ran into a *Twilight* cast-member on the street, so I was a little too nervous to take it, but I still wonder what it was.'

Like Taylor, Anna has found that being in *Twilight* has opened up lots of doors for her. In between *Twilight* and *New Moon* being filmed, she was cast as Natalie Keener in *Up in the Air* alongside George Clooney. She did so well that she was nominated for a Best Supporting Actress Oscar for her performance. She released a statement on 2 February 2010 saying: 'I am thrilled beyond words to be nominated with these talented and inspiring women. Being involved in a film as special as *Up in the Air* was a dream come true. I am overwhelmed and honored by this nomination and am so grateful to be able to share this experience with George [Clooney], Vera [Farmiga] and [director] Jason [Reitman].'

Ashley Greene

The actress who plays Alice Cullen in the *Twilight Saga* movies is Ashley Greene. Her on-screen character might hate Taylor's character but in real life the two get on

TAYLOR'S FRIENDS AND *TWILIGHT* CO-STARS, ASHLEY GREENE AND KELLAN LUTZ.

really well. Ashley might be five years older than Taylor, but she was a lot less experienced than him when she turned up on the *Twilight* set. She had only had minor roles in TV shows and films, playing a 'girlfriend' and a 'McDonald's customer', so had never had an opportunity to shine. Like Taylor, it was in *New Moon* that the audience began to realise that Ashley could really act.

Ashley thinks that Taylor looks amazing now that he's got his muscles. She told *In Touch*: 'He looks like he's in *300*! I was in the make-up trailer and I looked over as he was taking his shirt off and said to him, "You've got to be joking!" He looks fantastic. The girls are going to be satisfied, let me tell you!'

Ashley was one of the *Twilight* actors who really supported Taylor when it was suggested that he wouldn't be playing Jacob in *New Moon* because he didn't look old enough. In interviews, she was very vocal and suggested that if they got rid of Taylor then they should also get rid of her as she is quite a bit taller than Alice is supposed to be, according to Stephenie Meyer's books.

She told MTV back then: 'We all love Taylor – he's the best kid. He's so adorable and so good-hearted, and he's a good actor too. He did a great job, so I'm hoping to see him come back.

'I love him to death, and he'll grow – I know he's working out like crazy to try to bulk up. I think there are a lot of people [in *Twilight*] who don't necessarily physically fit their part, so I'm hoping we keep him.'

Ashley must have been so proud that day when she saw Taylor with his shirt off. He had put everything on the line to play Jacob and it had paid off. She really enjoys acting alongside him so it would have been awful if another actor had been brought in to take his place.

Ashley loves shooting the scenes with Taylor when their characters insult each other. She told Fearnet.com: 'Those scenes are really fun to film! You know, they always say that the nicest people can play the meanest characters. I remember someone saying in an interview that Rachel McAdams was the sweetest girl, and she played this awful, mean character in *Mean Girls*. I think it's the same thing with Taylor. He's so sweet – I can look at him and be mean to him on-screen or have a fight with him, and know that he's not going to take it personally, so we definitely got to play off each other a little bit.'

Auditioning

Taylor might be one of the youngest members of the *Twilight* cast, but he has been to so many auditions that he has become a bit of an expert in performing well and showcasing his many talents there. He can still remember his very first audition when he was only seven years old.

Taylor explained to Mark Sells from *The Reel Deal*: 'The first audition that my karate instructor sent me out on was a Burger King commercial. It was kind of like a karate audition, in that they were basically looking for martial arts stuff. And they were looking for someone older, but he wanted to send me anyway to get the experience. So, I met with the casting director, we talked, and she asked for some poses. It was funny, though, because at the time I didn't even know what a pose was [laughing]! – I was only seven. But I learned quickly and did some poses for them. And I really liked it. I thought it went well, but I didn't get it.'

Taylor has always been a positive person and sees the best in things. He might not have been picked for the Burger King ad, but he was determined to keep going to auditions and not give up. Shortly afterwards, he committed himself to spending a month training in L.A. with Mike Chat to improve his skills. His family came too, and within a few weeks Taylor had an agent and a few more auditions under his belt.

He says of his time spent in L.A.: 'There were more auditions. I heard "no", "no", "no", "no", so many times. I got one call back; that gave me the drive to keep going. It happened on our very last day there.'

Once the month was over, Taylor moved back home

but he still made the long trip to L.A. whenever a good audition came up. This was sometimes a bit tricky because the time difference often meant that it was a race to get Taylor there so he wouldn't miss the opportunity.

As he explained to journalist Terri Finch Hamilton: 'They'd call at 9 or 10 at night, which was 6 or 7 their time, and say, "We've got an audition tomorrow – can you be here?" We'd leave really early in the morning and get there about noon. I'd go to the audition in the afternoon, take the red-eye [late-night flight] back to Grand Rapids, then go to school.'

Taylor had to make a lot of sacrifices to keep going to auditions as his home town was over 2,000 miles away; it was also very expensive, but his family wanted to support him and do what they could to help him become the great actor he could be. He was very lucky to have parents that were so loving and supportive.

Taylor has always been open about the way he prepares for auditions, and while promoting the 3-D movie, *The Adventures of Sharkboy and Lavagirl*, he was asked by eFilmCritic.com how he does it. He told them: 'When it comes to auditioning, I go through the script, go through the emotions that the writers want us to portray, and we go through them and into the audition and meet with the casting director. Sometimes when it's really big and it's a feature film, we meet with our acting coach for about an hour and go over the scene.'

Taylor has always made sure that in every audition he gives his all by researching the roles and spending time getting to understand each character that he is asked to play. When it came to *Twilight* things were a bit different because he hadn't actually read any of Stephenie Meyer's books before he auditioned. This meant he only had a limited knowledge of who Jacob was and what he stood for. Robert Pattinson, on the other hand, *had* read *Twilight* but he felt like he couldn't play Edward because he wasn't good-looking enough. Ultimately, both Taylor and Robert turned out to be the best actors to bring Stephenie's characters from the page to the big screen.

Taylor told Abbey Simmons from Buddytv.com: 'The only thing is that they needed sides for me to read, so they used the beach scene from the movie, from the script, and then I had two other scenes and they literally just pulled quotes from *New Moon* and *Eclipse* and made them sides. So I actually got to do a couple scenes from *New Moon* and *Eclipse* with Kristen. It was kind of fun, it was a little taste.'

Twilight director Catherine Hardwicke took Taylor and the rest of the shortlisted actors back to her house for their final audition to find out who would be the best for each role. She made Taylor do a scene from *New Moon* in her backyard, Robert Pattinson and Kristen Stewart had to do a kissing scene in her bedroom and they also had to act out the biology scene in her dining

Taylor and Kristen at the Berlin prèmiere of *Twilight: Eclipse*

room. Taylor and Robert showed great chemistry with Kristen, so Catherine knew she had found the perfect Jacob and Edward.

Awards

You don't get to be as good an actor as Taylor without winning an award or two. In 2006, he was nominated for a Young Artist Award in the Best Performance in a Feature Film (Comedy or Drama) – Leading Young Actor category. It was for his role of Sharkboy in *The Adventures of Sharkboy and Lavagirl 3-D*. Sadly, he didn't win and was beaten by Josh Hutcherson, who plays Walter in *Zathura: A Space Adventure* (Josh has gone on to play Steve in *Cirque du Freak: The Vampire's Assistant* and Sean in *Adventure at the Center of the Earth*).

It took three years for Taylor to receive another nomination but since then he hasn't stopped being nominated and invited to a whole host of different awards shows. In 2009, he was nominated for an MTV Movie Award for Breakthrough Performance Male for playing Jacob in *Twilight* and he won a 'Teen Choice Award' in the Choice Movie Fresh Face Male category too. 2010 looks set to be an even bigger year for Taylor as he has already been nominated for a 'Saturn Award' from the Academy of Science Fiction,

TAYLOR ON THE RED
CARPET AT THE MTV
MOVIE AWARDS IN 2009.

Fantasy & Horror Films, and another Young Artist Award too. He was thrilled to be nominated for three People's Choice Awards and couldn't believe it when he won two – the award for Favourite Breakout Actor and Favourite Onscreen Team with Kristen Stewart and Robert Pattinson.

Winning the Favourite Male Actor category at the Nickelodeon Kids' Choice Awards in March 2010 was a dream come true for Taylor. He was up against some big names – Zac Efron, Shia LaBeouf and Tyler Perry – but he still managed to come out on top. Taylor has always wanted one of the orange trophies and in his acceptance speech he thanked his fans and said he was sharing the award with them. How sweet!

Backstage, he told reporters: 'I can't believe it! I was just honoured to just be in the category with everyone else; I can't believe it, I'm still dazed. This whole awards show is about the kids – they run it, it's amazing and I'm just so thankful to have all of them behind us.'

He also enjoyed talking to *Iron Man* star Robert Downey Jr. and Will Smith while he was there. Maybe one day he might get the opportunity to act alongside them in a big blockbuster.

Taylor has some huge movies coming out in 2010 and 2011, so he must be in the running for quite a few more awards. His mum might have to get him a trophy cabinet or something for his room so he can keep all his awards together and look at them when he gets the chance to visit home. He is so busy at the moment, running from one movie set to the next, that he can't really take them all with him.

B is for...

Bad Habits

Taylor might seem the perfect guy, but he insists that he isn't and that he does do things that annoy people. He says his worst bad habit is that he bounces his knees. He explained to *Seventeen* magazine: 'I bounce my knees, but I do not have Restless Leg Syndrome. I did an interview – I don't even know who it was with – and they said I told them I have Restless Leg Syndrome and it distracts me from my work. I do not have a syndrome, I actually have many friends who just bounce their knees.'

Taylor can't help getting his knees to bounce when he sits down – he just can't sit still. Sometimes people get annoyed and Taylor notices, so he tries to stop it from happening by pressing down on his knees with his hands, but it doesn't work: they just keep on bouncing. Taylor isn't too concerned because it feels natural and so interviewers will just have to put up with his 'worst bad habit.'

Beach Bowl

On 6 February 2010, Taylor took part in the 4th Annual DIRECTV Celebrity Beach Bowl. It's a flag football match that's held on South Beach, Miami, during Super Bowl Week each year. Fans that were there or watched it on TV saw Taylor play with and against huge stars like Jennifer Lopez, Chace Crawford and Kellan Lutz. Each team had some American football legends playing, too.

Taylor was interviewed during the event and asked how good he is at football. He replied: 'I played for eight years, I was a running back: we'll have to see – I haven't played in a little bit.' He also told them that he wanted to be a star and not get hurt.

In fact, Taylor did really well and was one of the best players. He was incredibly fast and his opposition players had to work hard to catch up with him. Taylor did so well, considering the match was played on sand and he'd have to work harder – it's a good job he's so fit.

TAYLOR TAKES PART IN CELEBRITY BEACH BOWL IN MIAMI.

Beards

You won't see Taylor with a beard anytime soon. Robert Pattinson might like walking around unshaven when he's not playing Edward, but you'll never come across Taylor with stubble. He shaves three or four times a week, which keeps him looking smart and sexy.

Our favourite actor isn't at all vain and only looks in the mirror once or twice a day. He says he really should have played one of the vampires in *Twilight* because he doesn't

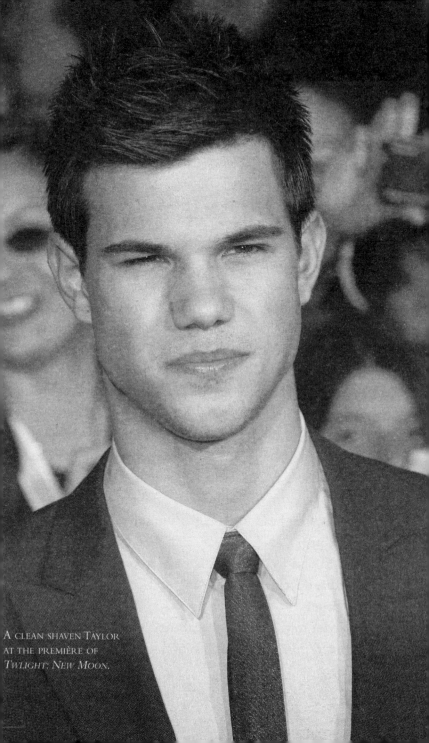

A CLEAN SHAVEN TAYLOR
AT THE PREMIÈRE OF
TWILIGHT: NEW MOON.

tan, but burns instead. Taylor says he isn't a drinker and would rather have a bottle of water than a bottle of wine – he's certainly a good role model for young boys.

Bedroom

Having spent the last couple of years living out of a suitcase, Taylor must miss his bedroom back home. He has been so busy filming *Twilight*, *New Moon*, *Eclipse*, *My Own Worst Enemy* and *Valentine's Day* that he hasn't spent much time at home. With the *Twilight* movies being so popular, he has stayed in some of the best hotels around the world. He has travelled to Australia, Japan and Germany – there are not many places Taylor hasn't been to promote *Twilight*.

Taylor and the rest of the *Twilight* cast do their best to make their hotel rooms as homely as possible. With each movie, their rooms have been upgraded so they have more space to chill-out after filming wraps each day. Usually, they head to Robert Pattinson's room because he has a piano and a guitar, and they can jam together. Robert and Jackson Rathbone like to play guitar, Nikki Reed and Kristen Stewart sing, and Taylor prefers playing the drums.

Taylor told *Seventeen* magazine: 'I've always kind of had an interest in the drums but nothing else. The drums are the only thing I feel I would be good at, because I'm a very physical person. I've always played sports and stuff – drums would give me something to do.'

It would be great if the *Breaking Dawn* soundtrack could have a few tracks on it that the cast have recorded together.

Best Friends

Taylor loves spending time with his best friends, but you won't find him talking about them in interviews. He likes to keep his private life private. Because lots of Taylor's friends aren't famous, he won't reveal their names in interviews; if he did, they would have *Twilight* fans camping outside their homes, desperate to be introduced to Taylor.

Taylor told Terri Finch Hamilton from *The Grand Rapids Press* that he stayed a normal, grounded student when he was in school, even though he was getting acting jobs. He admitted: 'Kids still looked at me as Taylor, because they knew me from before. You gotta remember who your friends were before you got famous.' That way he can avoid those people who 'suddenly want to be your best friend.'

Having friends who aren't famous helps Taylor keep his feet on the ground and not believe his own hype. As he explained on the *Lopez Tonight* Show: 'I spend time with the same people – I spend time with my family and my friends before I've made new friends, which is fantastic, but I think it's just a matter of surrounding yourself with that inner group.'

Birthdays

Turning 18 on 11 February 2010 was very important to Taylor, but he didn't want to have a big celebrity party. He just wanted to celebrate with the people he loves most.

Taylor was very open with *Access Hollywood* when they asked him what he had planned. He told them: 'Absolutely nothing, really! I mean, I'll spend time with family and friends. I don't like to do anything huge, but it *is* eighteen, so it's kind of a big one, I guess.'

On the day itself he was snapped by the paparazzi leaving his local gym after a workout. He must be really committed to looking buff, if he even exercises on his birthday – not many people would do that.

As well as it being an important day for Taylor, it was a big day for his fans too. They sent him birthday cards – some even posted them a month early to make sure he got them on time – and held their own special birthday parties in his honour. The restaurants in his local area were packed to the rafters with fans having their own '18-Tay Day' celebrations. Things nearly got

Taylor has a very close relationship with his fans.

out of hand when a fan posted that Taylor was enjoying an ice-cream sundae at a Des Moines, Iowa Tastee Freez. Hundreds of fans turned up and tried to get in, but it's still not known whether Taylor was there or if this was actually a hoax.

Bodyguards

Taylor might try and live as normal a life as possible but he still needs to have bodyguards when he attends big events. Fans would never want to hurt Taylor but sometimes bodyguards are necessary to help keep the crowds back and stop Taylor from getting crushed. They are also needed on set to keep the paparazzi photographers from hassling Taylor and allow him to film his scenes without being interrupted.

Some fans get frustrated when they try to give his bodyguards letters and gifts to pass on to Taylor, but they refuse to take them. They can't understand why the bodyguards are so mean. These fans need to understand that the bodyguards have to say no because they must concentrate on what they are doing – protecting Taylor. They don't have time to take presents to him and it certainly isn't safe to do so – they might be given something that could harm Taylor by someone pretending to be a fan.

If you want to write to Taylor, you can. The address you need is:

Taylor Lautner
c/o William Morris Agency
One William Morris Place
Beverly Hills,
California
90212
USA.

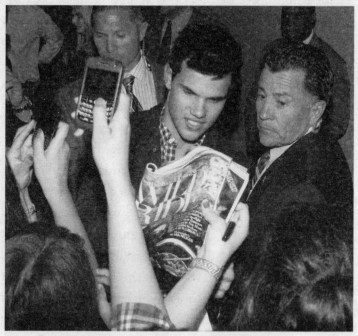

TAYLOR IS HAPPY TO SIGN AUTOGRAPHS FOR HIS FANS.

It's best if you enclose a self-addressed envelope too. Please be patient because Taylor gets a lot of fan mail, so it might be six months or so before you hear anything back. You can send him letters, cards and small gifts if you like. Some fan sites send Taylor fantastic keepsake books filled with lovely messages from his fans.

Books

Taylor could never be described as a bookworm because he has never been a great fan of books. He would much rather play computer games than settle down to enjoy a novel, but when he read *Twilight* for the first time he was pleasantly surprised.

He told *Rolling Stone* magazine: 'I admit proudly that I enjoyed the series. I was not a book reader at all. But then when I read them, they hook you. I feel like each book, and more so the movies, are just getting more exciting, and better and better. With *New Moon*, you know, it's not just the love story between these two anymore. Now there are three people, and it's dangerous.'

Robert Pattinson and Kristen Stewart might think that *New Moon* is the best book in the series, but Taylor disagrees with them. He loved *Eclipse* the most and so he couldn't wait to get started on filming it as soon as *New Moon* wrapped.

STEPHENIE MEYER AT THE SIGNING OF TAYLOR'S FAVOURITE *TWILIGHT* BOOK, *ECLIPSE*.

When Taylor's agent first suggested that he should audition for *Twilight*, the actor had no idea what it was about or that it was based on a series of books. He had never seen a *Twilight* book in a bookstore, but then again he didn't really visit them.

Taylor admitted to journalist Abbey Simmons: 'As soon as I was cast, that was when I found out how big this was and what the potential was. I was so excited to be a part of it. I was like "Wow!" Originally I was just excited to work with Catherine Hardwicke and I did a chemistry read with Kristen Stewart and so I was excited to work with them. But then when I found out how much of a phenomenon this was, it was crazy for me.'

Taylor and millions of fans worldwide might think that *Twilight* author Stephenie Meyer is a talented writer, but not everyone in the literary world agrees. Award-winning author Stephen King told an interviewer from *USA Weekend*: 'Jo Rowling [*Harry Potter*] is a terrific writer and Stephenie Meyer can't write worth a darn – she's not very good.'

Ouch! Taylor completely disagrees. He loves the way Stephenie wrote Jacob, especially in *Twilight* and *New Moon*.

Taylor divulged to Naibe Reynoso from ReelzChannel: '[Jacob's] very interesting. I love the way Stephenie wrote him in the first movie – you know, he's a Native American. He's very friendly and easy to talk with, then in the second one it becomes interesting because, you know, he turns into a werewolf and what I find cool is like, he has this Native American side, who's just this happy-go-lucky kid, then he has this werewolf side where, you know, he's trying to hold back his temper and he wants to be violent.'

Breaking Dawn

The final book of the *Twilight Saga* is *Breaking Dawn* and when the last movie of the series comes out, this will be the last time we get to see Taylor as Jacob Black. When *Twilight* became a big box-office hit and it was announced that *New Moon* and *Eclipse* would be made into movies, fans everywhere were ecstatic. They were thrilled that the movies would get bigger budgets too, but were keener to find out whether *Breaking Dawn* would be given the green light – and they had to wait a long time to find out.

It was Robert Pattinson who finally let the cat out of the bag while promoting *New Moon*. In a press conference he confirmed that *Breaking Dawn* the movie was going to happen and that it would probably be filmed in the fall of 2010.

On 10th June 2010 it was announced that there would be two *Breaking Dawn* movies. The first is due to be released in November 2011 and the second in 2012.

Turning the book *Breaking Dawn* into a single movie would have caused quite a few headaches for the director and screenwriter because there's a lot to try and cram into two and a half hours. If they had made the movie any longer some fans might have found it too difficult to sit through without needing toilet breaks! The *Breaking Dawn* story will also be difficult to film because it contains quite a lot of adult content that might prevent young *Twilight* fans from seeing it.

If you haven't read *Breaking Dawn* yet, here is a short summary. In the first part of the book, Bella and Edward get married and Bella becomes pregnant. Then, in the second part, the Quileute wolf pack believes the baby poses an unknown threat and so they decide to kill Bella and her unborn child. Jacob objects and leaves to form his own pack with Seth and Leah, however. Bella gives birth, but in doing so, breaks most of the bones in her body and loses so much blood that Edward is forced to change her into a vampire before she dies. Jacob witnesses the birth and imprints on baby Renesmee.

In the third part of the book, Bella and Edward start to raise their daughter but things take a turn for the worse when vampire Irina wrongly believes that Renesmee is an immortal child and reports her to the Volturi. They take the same view and decide to destroy Renesmee and the Cullens. Edward, Bella and the rest of the Cullens gather other vampire clans to testify to the Volturi that

Renesmee is not an immortal child. When the Volturi realise that Irina is wrong, they destroy her but still consider getting rid of Renesmee, thinking she might still be a threat to the secret existence of vampires. Before they can do so, Alice and Jasper return with Nahuel, a 150-year-old vampire human crossbreed, who proves that crossbreeds pose no threat. The Volturi accept his testimony and Edward, Bella and Renesmee are sent home safe in the knowledge that the Volturi no longer seek to destroy them.

In April 2010, the *Twilight* screenwriter Melissa Rosenberg was asked whether *Breaking Dawn* could be made into a PG-13 movie (12A in the UK) because of the vampire sex and gruesome birth in Stephenie Meyer's book. Melissa told Film.com: 'That's your audience – in this series you don't sacrifice anything. There are some movies that wouldn't play at PG-13, like *The Hangover*, but this is just not one of them for me. Again, if you're capturing character, emotion and emotional journey, you're OK.'

In the same interview, Melissa also talked about our favourite leading man. She told the reporter: 'Taylor Lautner is a rare breed. He wanted something, and he made it happen. It could easily have gone the other way: if he doesn't do anything, maybe it doesn't happen for him. [He's] incredibly driven. That character is such a physical character that it had to be a transformation.'

twilight saga

lipse

07.10

BELLA AND JACOB'S
RELATIONSHIP IS TESTED
TO THE LIMITS IN THE
FINAL 2 FILMS OF THE
TWILIGHT SAGA.

When the final *Breaking Dawn* movie wraps, it's going to be a sad time for *Twilight* fans everywhere. This will be the last time that we will get to see Taylor as Jacob Black, Kristen as Bella Swan and Robert as Edward Cullen.

We might have to say goodbye to Jacob Black at the end of *Breaking Dawn*, but we won't have to bid farewell to Taylor – he's going to be making great movies for a very long time.

Bullying

Taylor hates bullies and would never bully anyone himself. Despite having amazing martial arts skills, he would never fight someone who hit him – he knows that violence is not the answer and would calmly walk away.

When Taylor was in school some of his schoolmates were jealous of his acting career and tried to make him feel like he was worthless. Taylor did his best to ignore the horrible things they said to him.

He revealed to *Rolling Stone* magazine: 'I was never extremely confident. Because I was an actor when I was in school there was a little bullying going on. Not physical bullying, but people making fun of what I do. I just had to tell myself: I can't let this get to me. This is what I love to do and I'm going to continue to do it.'

Taylor did so well not to react to what the bullies said

to him. It would have been awful if he had hit one of them because he might have been expelled from school.

In the future it would be nice if Taylor could team up with Robert Pattinson, who was also bullied when he was at school, and do something for an anti-bullying charity. Taylor is a great role model and has proved that the bullies were wrong – he's definitely worth something! Right now, the kids who bullied him are probably really jealous of his success when they see him on TV or attending big movie premières – they must wish they'd been nicer to him when they were growing up.

C is for...

Cancun

We are going to see an even sexier version of Taylor than we see in the *Twilight* movies when he stars in his next project, *Cancun*. For Taylor, this must be a dream movie as it will be his first full-on action role. It will be released in 2011, if Taylor's schedule allows it to be filmed sometime in 2010.

This is a really exciting part for Taylor as he gets to play a super-fit college student, who is on a spring break trip to Cancun with some friends when the others are kidnapped and held hostage by a Mexican drug cartel kingpin. He has to find them, fight the baddies and bring them home without being killed himself.

TAYLOR WILL HOPEFULLY BE TAKING ON MORE AND MORE ROLES FOLLOWING *TWILIGHT*.

It will be a Summit Entertainment film in conjunction with Temple Hill. Summit are the studio behind the *Twilight* movies and the Robert Pattinson film, *Remember Me*. Taylor's dad Dan will be involved too, as the movie is to be produced under Taylor Made Entertainment.

Taylor Made Entertainment is a production company formed by Dan Lautner for Taylor so that they can develop great movie and TV roles together for him to do. Robert Pattinson has always wanted his own production company, so it's funny that Taylor has beaten him to it, even though Robert is actually six years older than him.

Catherine Hardwicke

Catherine Hardwicke is the fantastic director who directed *Twilight* and made it a massive hit. Many people might credit Stephenie Meyer for coming up with the original story or say that it's down to Robert, Taylor and Kristen that the movie became such a big hit, but really, it was Catherine who brought all the elements together.

Catherine was the one who stuck her neck out and objected to the first *Twilight* script she was given. She could have kept quiet, but she thought changes were necessary.

The director told *Time* magazine what the first *Twilight* script was like: 'Bella was a track star. Then there were FBI agents – the vampires would migrate south into Mexico every year, and FBI agents in Utah were tracking them. They ended up on an island, chasing everyone around on jet skis.'

Catherine read all of Stephenie Meyer's books; she began to imagine how great the movie could be, if only it stuck to the story. Soon she got in touch with a great screenwriter called Melissa Rosenberg and together they wrote the second script.

One of the main reasons why Taylor wanted to be in *Twilight* was because Catherine would be directing it. She had directed the award-winning movies *Thirteen* and *The Nativity Story*. In fact, Catherine wrote *Thirteen* in six days with Nikki Reed (who went on to play Rosalie in the *Twilight* movies).

Catherine was the first female director that Taylor had worked for and she was nothing like how he had expected her to be. He told Rebecca Murray from Movies.About.com: 'Catherine's such a ball to be around – she's just a goofy kid. It's funny because I wasn't expecting that. I was expecting: this is like a dark, intense drama film, we've got to have some hardcore, yelling director, but not at all.'

From his first audition Taylor just knew that Catherine would be amazing to work with because she had energy, a deep desire for the story and was very enthusiastic and optimistic. As he explained to journalist Abbey Simmons:

CATHERINE HARDWICKE ATTENDS A PREMIÈRE WITH *TWILIGHT* ACTRESS CHRISTIAN SERRATOS.

'It's that sort of energy that brings great performances out of young actors who are operating on a more energetic level. She actually has that energetic level, so she works well with young people and you know that from her previous work, like *Lords of Dogtown* and *Thirteen*. She has a great history with younger actors – I think that's one of the unique things she brings, as well as her design background. She has a great eye; an eye for space and action. She's talented.'

Taylor had such a great working relationship with Catherine that he could tell her when he thought that she was doing something wrong. By then, he had read *Twilight* so many times that he knew which scenes the fans would want to have in the movie – especially those key scenes that involved Jacob Black. But when he read the original script and saw that Jacob wasn't included in the prom scene he was quite shocked as it was an important part of the book. Taylor said: 'When I read the script I was like, "Really, he doesn't come to the prom?"'

'I think I asked Catherine about it and I forget what she said. But I was just like, "Oh, okay..." But sure enough, you know, they were like, "Okay, we're doing it."'

It's great that Taylor got to do the prom scene – it really adds something to the movie because it shows the tension between Jacob and Edward.

Cayden Boyd

When Taylor was filming *The Adventures of Sharkboy and Lavagirl 3-D* he became really friendly with Cayden Boyd. Cayden played Max, the boy who dreams up Planet Drool and his favourite dream superheroes, Sharkboy and Lavagirl.

Taylor talked about his friendship with Cayden and Taylor Dooley (who played Lavagirl) to Mark Sells from the *Oregon Herald* during a promotional tour for the movie. He said: 'We had a lot of fun on the set, with Cayden too. After we were done shooting, the three of us would go behind the set and play hide-n-seek and climb trees – we had so much fun on the set. And we all see each other a lot since we live only a few blocks from one another. We go out to dinner together and we have many of our friends from the set over for sleepovers.'

Taylor has always been a bit of a joker and likes having fun with the people he works with. Robert Pattinson is much more serious and prefers to cut himself off from the rest of the *Twilight* cast in order to truly get in character. Taylor is more relaxed and everyone who works with him says he's great to be around.

Taylor admitted: 'We played jokes on Cayden all the time. You see, he's a big Aggie fan and we were shooting on the University of Texas campus. And of course, UT and

Texas A&M have a huge rivalry. So, we'd have lots of fun with him. There was a dog on the set named Tippy and we'd put UT stickers and a UT collar on her, and would say that it was UT's new mascot. We also went back and forth, posting different messages and stuff on our doors. And I just remember all those kinds of moments on the set. It was a very family-friendly environment.'

It's great that Taylor's early acting experiences were such good fun. He made some really firm friendships that are still going strong, many years later. Since *The Adventures of Sharkboy and Lavagirl 3-D*, Cayden's acting career continues to flourish and he has starred as Young Angel in *X-Men: The Last Stand* and alongside Hayden Panettiere in *Fireflies in the Garden*. Hopefully, one day he'll act alongside Taylor again and they can go on new adventures together!

Chaske Spencer

The super-talented actor who plays werewolf Sam Uley in the *Twilight* movies is called Chaske Spencer. He was thrilled to be cast as one of Taylor's on-screen buddies and they get on really well in real life too, even though he is nearly double Taylor's age.

Robert Pattinson and the other Cullen actors tend to hang round together, while Taylor and the wolf pack often

Cayden met Taylor on the set of *The Adventures of Sharkboy and Lavagirl 3-D.*

head to the gym to work out and then catch up with the others over dinner.

Chaske explained to *Seventeen* magazine what it's like to be working with Taylor: 'Taylor is a lovable man! He is so cool! First, he is raised right. He is a good kid, he's got his head on his shoulders and he's fun. He can be an adult when it comes to work, but he is still 17, so he can be a kid as well. He gets really bored easily, so between takes he will do flips and stuff. And he can do break-dancing and karate. The production people had to tell him to chill a few times because it got a little rowdy.'

He also talked about what the wolf pack did on set while filming *New Moon* and *Eclipse*: 'We goofed around a lot. It's really fun because you get to hang out with these guys that you get along with. It was like a party — we would all pile into my trailer and watch a movie sometimes, if it was taking a while to get to set or if they were busy filming something else. On off time, we would go to restaurants and clubs together. They were like my brothers.'

It's so great that Taylor has his own crew to hang out with when the Cullen actors are off shooting on another location. He can never get bored now he has Chaske, Alex Meraz [Paul], Bronson Pelletier [Jared] and Kiowa Gordon [Embry] for company.

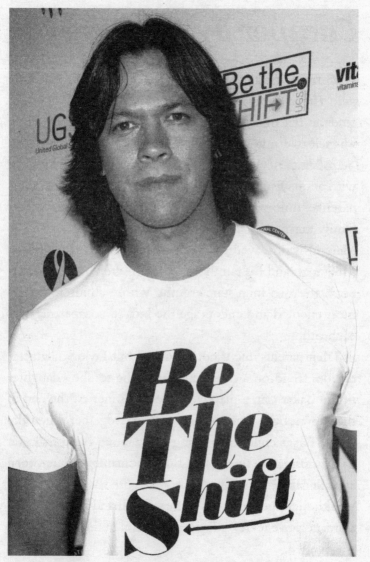

CHASKE SPENCER PLAYED SAM ULEY IN THE *TWILIGHT* SAGA.

Cheaper by the Dozen 2

2005 was a really busy year for Taylor because not only did *The Adventures of Sharkboy and Lavagirl 3-D* hit cinemas but his other big movie, *Cheaper by the Dozen 2*, was released just after Christmas.

In *Cheaper by the Dozen 2* Taylor plays Eliot Murtaugh, with actors Eugene Levy and Carmen Electra playing his parents, Jimmy and Sarina. In the movie, the Baker family travel to Lake Winnetka and Tom Baker (Steve Martin) is dismayed to discover that his old rival Jimmy Murtaugh and his family of eight children are there, too. Soon the two men start arguing whose children are the most talented and encourage the kids to compete against each other.

Their parents might not get along, but Taylor's character decides to go on a date with Sarah, the tomboy daughter in the Baker clan – played by Alyson Stoner. At the end of the movie, both families have to work together when the oldest Baker child starts going into labour. Nora makes it to the hospital in the nick of time and names the newborn after her father, Tom.

Although the film wasn't a massive hit and received quite a few negative reviews, Taylor's portrayal of the lovable Eliot was praised.

Chris Weitz

When *Twilight* director Catherine Hardwicke turned down the opportunity to direct *New Moon*, fans of the series were shocked. They couldn't understand why she didn't want to direct Taylor, Kristen and Robert again. Although she had been offered a lot of money to do the second movie, she turned it down not because she didn't want to take on the next *Twilight* project, but because she thought she wouldn't be able to do it justice. She didn't feel like there would be enough time to prepare because Summit bosses wanted filming to start just a few months later so the movie could be released in November 2009.

As soon as Catherine said no, Summit had to find an equally talented director who could make *New Moon* into an amazing movie. They found their man in Chris Weitz.

Once he was signed up, Chris wrote in an email to *Twilight* fans everywhere: 'Like many of you, I am a fan of Catherine Hardwicke's work. I can't really say much about why she is not doing *New Moon* because I wasn't involved in those decisions, but I can say that I will devote myself to making the very best and most faithful version of *New Moon* that can be brought to the screen. To those who doubt that as a male director I can capture Bella's experience, I can only say that emotion is universal and that my work has often involved working with some of the most talented actresses in the world.'

Chris Weitz was the director of *The Golden Compass* and the Hugh Grant flick, *About a Boy*. In addition to producing more than a dozen films and TV shows, he has even been an actor too, so he knows what it's like to be on the other side of the camera. Stephenie Meyer was really excited when Chris agreed to direct *New Moon* because *About a Boy* is one of her favourite movies of all time and not only did Chris direct it, but he wrote the screenplay too.

Taylor nearly didn't get the opportunity to work with Chris as originally it was thought that another actor would be brought in to play Jacob – Taylor was viewed by many as being too small and slight to play Jacob when he transforms in *New Moon*. But Taylor worked so hard to build himself up that Chris had no hesitation in telling him that he *would* be playing Jacob in *New Moon*.

On her website Stephenie Meyer published the statement that Chris had released to show his support of Taylor so that all *Twilight* fans could read it. In it, he said: 'I'm very happy to announce that Taylor Lautner will be playing Jacob Black in *New Moon* and that he's doing so with the enthusiastic support of Summit Entertainment, the producers, and Stephenie Meyer.

'The characters in Stephenie's books go through extraordinary changes of circumstance and also appearance;

New Moon director Chris Weitz lines up with the stars of the film.

so it is not surprising that there has been speculation about whether the same actor would portray a character who changes in so many surprising ways throughout the series. But it was my first instinct that Taylor was, is, and should be Jacob, and that the books would be best served by the actor who is emotionally right for the part. I think that fans of *Twilight* the book and the movie will be surprised by the Jacob Black that Taylor will bring to the screen in *New Moon*; and I'm looking forward to working with him and the rest of the cast in realizing the film.'

Stephenie added her own little statement, too: 'I'd just like to add that I was very much a part of this decision. My first priority was always what was best for *New Moon* – what was going to give us the best possible movie. I'm truly thrilled that Taylor was the one who proved to the director, to Summit, and to me that he is the best possible Jacob we could have. And I'm very much looking forward to seeing what he's going to bring to Jacob's character this year.'

Taylor was so glad that Chris gave him the chance to play Jacob Black again and he really enjoyed working with him in the months that followed. He told Talia Soghomonian from Metro News: 'Chris is amazing. He's extremely talented and he's done a lot of amazing work. Everything is looking fantastic so far for this and I know it's going to continue. But at the same time, the set is so calm and relaxed and we're just having a really great time.

Sometimes you wonder, "How is he doing this? How is he creating this beautiful work and we're just all having a blast doing it?" Chris has definitely taken control and he's a blast to be around.'

Asked to compare Catherine Hardwicke and Chris Weitz, Taylor told Hitfix.com: 'They're both so talented in different ways. What I love about Chris is the set is very calm and we're just having a lot of fun making the movie. And then you sit back, and you look at the results that are happening and it looks amazing so far. I'm so excited to see it. And you just sit back and see what's going on, and you're like, "How are we having such an easygoing, relaxed time making this movie, and it's turning out the way it is?" At the same time, the conversations with Catherine – she just related to us so well. So does Chris. They're both talented directors, and I'm thankful that I had the opportunity to work with both of them.'

In the beginning, it was actually the opportunity of working with Taylor, Kristen and Robert that made Chris want to do the movie. He revealed what motivated him to *Entertainment Weekly*: 'I really liked the actors. I saw the first movie and I thought there was something special about Kristen, Rob, and Taylor. I liked the emotional tones to the book. It was stuff I knew how to do. I had this theory that if you stay true to the book, you would win. You would not only win with the fans, but other people will get what the fans care about. If the box office tells us anything, then it's a win. It's made more in its first day than the entire domestic run of *Golden Compass*. It's extraordinary.'

Chris is a big fan of Taylor and says that one of his happiest times on set was when Taylor realised that he was going to be able to pull off Jacob at the start of filming. Chris has said this was very gratifying for him. He thinks the scene where Jacob jumps into Bella's room is Taylor's best one: 'There is so much pathos there, even though it's melodrama, there's something touching about it. Or maybe the last moment he has, just when he says Bella's name. You sort of understand just how crushed he is at that moment. There are a few times where he's absolutely that guy and it's really lovely. He's that guy for the fans and that's what I always thought he could do.'

Clothes

Taylor is one of the most fashionable young men on the planet. It doesn't matter what he wears – he still looks so hot. When his workout regime for *New Moon* started, Taylor had to get himself a whole new wardrobe because he outgrew all his clothes. He went from a small man's size to a large in a matter of weeks.

When Taylor's relaxing, he likes to wear simple T-shirts

and jeans with trainers. He isn't afraid to show off a bit of his chest, though, so often the T-shirts have a V-neck or a few buttons undone. For award shows he likes to dress smart-casual, so usually wears a white shirt, black trousers and a trendy waistcoat or jacket. He doesn't wear trainers like Robert Pattinson but instead opts for stylish black shoes.

To premières and fan events he wears designer suits that show off his fine figure. They are cut perfectly to make the most of his muscles. For the Oscars he had to wear a black tuxedo – Taylor really is the sexiest guy in Hollywood!

Lots of celebrities bring out their own fashion ranges, so in the future we might see clothes designed by Taylor for sale in the stores. They would be really popular as people already rush out and buy the clothes that they see Taylor in.

Taylor might be very stylish but he doesn't really understand female fashion. When he was asked by *Seventeen* magazine which girl fashion trend confuses him, he admitted: 'I have one that sometimes I don't understand and sometimes I think is really cute: leg warmers. Sometimes it looks really awkward, like "Why are you wearing those?" and sometimes it's like, "That's pretty cute!" Maybe it's the girl or has something to do with wearing them on a sunny day – like when its California weather and its 90 degrees, you don't need to be wearing them. Maybe that's the answer: the fashion trend I don't understand – leg warmers when it's 90 degrees out!'

Comic-Con

Comic-Con is an annual fan convention held in San Diego, which showcases comic books, science fiction/fantasy, film and television. It was at Comic-Con that Taylor and the rest of the *Twilight* cast first realised how big the *Twilight* fan base was and how their lives were about to be changed forever.

Taylor revealed all about his experiences of Comic-Con 2008 to Adrienne Gaffney from *Vanity Fair*: 'First of all, Comic-Con was crazy. I knew it was going to be. They had told me, "This is a big event and there's going to be like 6,000 fans there." We got there and it was huge. Just coming out on stage and hearing everyone scream and seeing how many people were in that auditorium was crazy.'

There were actually 125,000 *Twilight* fans at Comic-Con, who all wanted to be in the room with Taylor, Kristen and Rob, but only 6,000 lucky fans managed to fit in. The others just had to queue up in the hope that they could grab themselves a photo with Taylor when he came out or even a quick autograph. Sadly, many of them didn't get their wish because there was no way that Taylor

Taylor and Kristen turn out for the annual Comic-Con in San Diego.

could sign so many autographs – it would have taken him weeks to get through them all.

But Taylor and the rest of the *Twilight* cast couldn't spend all their time at Comic-Con with the fans – they had to do lots of press interviews too. In total, Taylor had to do 77 – he must have been so tired by the time he left.

Taylor's second experience of Comic-Con was busier than his first. Because he had a much bigger role in *New Moon*, a lot more questions were fired at him and he had to do many more interviews. When shown clips from the movie of Taylor without his top on, everyone went crazy. Robert Pattinson was no longer the number 1 *Twilight* hunk – now it was Taylor's name that the fans were chanting.

Competitions

Less than three years after Taylor started to learn karate, his teacher decided that he was good enough to compete in competitions. He entered Taylor into a championship set in Louisville, but no one expected Taylor to do as well as he did.

He managed to come out on top in three disciplines. Wow!

One of the best martial arts competitors on the planet,

Mike Chat, was watching and he wanted to help Taylor become even better – he knew that with his help Taylor could become a world champion.

 Dance

Taylor gets quite embarrassed whenever anyone mentions dancing because he doesn't see himself as a dancer. He would much rather talk about his acting career or his love of sport.

But there was a time when he would talk quite openly about dancing. When he was promoting *The Adventures of Sharkboy and Lavagirl 3-D*, he told Michael J. Lee from RadioFree: 'Yeah, I do hip-hop dancing, and I've been doing that for, like, a year and a half. But the karate – I don't compete anymore, I just train at my house to keep up the skill.'

As well as a great actor and karate champion, Taylor is also an amazing dancer.

We might not get to see Taylor's dancing skills in the *Twilight* movies, but we nearly had the chance of seeing them in *Fame*. Taylor auditioned for a part in the 2009 remake of the classic tale about students at a Performing Arts School, but he didn't get it. It's a real shame because it would have been nice to see him showing off his dancing and singing skills in a movie.

David Slade

While playing Jacob Black, David Slade was the third director that Taylor got to work with. David took over from Chris Weitz and put his own unique slant on the *Eclipse* story.

The first time Taylor met David he had no idea who he was. He was busy in a stunt rehearsal for *New Moon* when one of the producers, Wyck Godfrey, came in with someone that he had never seen before.

Taylor explained to Hitfix.com: 'Wyck was like, "Hey, this is David." And at that point he wasn't signed on to the film and I had no idea who he was. Then all of a sudden he started putting up these "camera hands" in my face: "Yeah, I think this would be a good angle right here." And I'm just sitting there, going, "What is he doing?" Then finally, as he's doing it, Wyck says, "Oh, I probably should tell you who this is. This is David Slade. He's probably going to be doing *Eclipse*." I was like, "Oh, that makes sense now!"'

Because filming on *Eclipse* started just a couple of months after *New Moon* wrapped, David Slade had to prepare while *New Moon* was being filmed. He went for a meal with the cast and Stephenie Meyer in Vancouver when *New Moon* finished and it's thought that he presented the cast with their new scripts that night. Some lucky fans managed to chat to David and he apologised for the negative things he might have said in the past about *Twilight* and gave them the peace sign.

David Slade probably had the hardest task out of all the directors in charge of a *Twilight* movie to win over the fans. Their problem with David started when he was asked on the *BDK Movie Show* which movie he was going to see, and he replied: '*Twilight* drunk? No, not even drunk! *Twilight* on acid? No, not even on acid! *Twilight* at gunpoint? Just shoot me!'

David was so concerned that the fans didn't like him that he sent an email to one of the biggest fan sites, Twilight Lexicon. In it, he stated: 'When I made these comments, I had neither seen the film nor read the books. I was promoting a comedy short film that I had made for *Xbox* and every pop culture subject was seen as a possible comedy target. I was being silly and none of the statements were from the heart.

'Of course, I have since seen the movie and read

DAVID SLADE DIRECTED THE THIRD *TWILIGHT* FILM, *ECLIPSE*.

the books, and was quickly consumed with the rich storytelling and the beautifully honest characters that Stephenie Meyer created. I would like to reassure everyone involved that I am invested in making the best film that I am humanly capable of, and that I am acutely aware of the power of the original books we serve.'

Taylor really loved filming *Eclipse* because it is his favourite book of the *Twilight Saga* and David Slade was a cool director to work with. He told VIP Access: 'I really enjoy the opportunity to work with different directors. It's challenging for us actors to adjust to different styles and it's cool just to watch and observe the different ways they work and their opinions on things. The cast – we're the same. We know these characters, we've been living them for a while together, so we have that dynamic over the established but it's really cool that we have a different director each time and see how they work with us.'

Driving

Initially, driving was going to be a problem for Taylor and Robert Pattinson because both were required to drive in the *Twilight Saga* movies, but neither of them had a licence. Robert could have been driving since the age of

17 but he had never learnt. In the parts of London where he lived it was much easier to jump on the Tube or to get on a bus than navigate along busy streets, trying to get a driving space, and so he'd never really had the inclination to get behind the wheel. In contrast, Taylor had been too young to drive but as soon as he was old enough, he set about learning so that he could drive in the movies.

Taylor proudly told Larry Carroll from MTV: 'I did recently get my driver's licence, yeah. Thank you. I've got my licence in my back pocket to show them I'm okay and that I won't kill them… hopefully.'

'I'm going to test out driving Bella's truck and my family's truck. One of them is an automatic, so that will be nice and easy. The other one has no power steering, so I'll have to muscle it. That will be interesting – I've never done that before.'

Taylor's dad really encouraged him to become confident behind the wheel. He spent hours in Bella's truck, helping Taylor to get used to it, so that it would look natural onscreen. He would do anything to help Taylor – he loves him so much and understood how important being able to drive was to his son. Indeed, Taylor would have hated it had a stunt double been pulled in to do his driving scenes.

TAYLOR TAKES TAYLOR SWIFT FOR A SPIN.

Duck Dodgers

After *The Adventures of Sharkboy and Lavagirl 3-D* hit cinemas, *Duck Dodgers* was Taylor's next project in 2005. It was an animated sci-fi cartoon series based on the alter ego of Daffy Duck: Duck Dodgers. Taylor provided the voice of Reggie Wasserstein in the episode titled 'A Lame Duck Mind' and the voice of Terrible Obnoxious Boy in the episode 'Good Duck Hunting/Consumption Overruled'.

It might not have been a massive role, but it was fun for Taylor to do something less taxing than a full-blown movie.

Above: Taylor's on-screen breakthrough came when he was just 13 and starred in *The Adventures of Sharkboy and Lavagirl*.

Below: Along with co-stars Kristen Stewart and Robert Pattinson, Taylor became a household name when he starred as Jacob Black in the *Twilight* saga.

Left: Cheeky Taylor has always enjoyed being in front of the camera.

Right: Taylor really disliked wearing a wig to play Jacob Black in the first *Twilight* film. He prefers to keep his hair short and spiky.

ylor played Christian Slater's son Jack Spivey in the short-lived television
ries, *My Own Worst Enemy*. He's pictured here with co-star, Bella Thorne.

Left: Taylor at the Los Angeles premier of the first *Twilight* film.

Below: Taylor and Taylor Swift are said to be 'just good friends'.

Taylor competes at the 4th
Annual DIRECTV Celebrity
Beach Bowl in Miami.

Taylor attends the
Golden Globe awards
in Los Angeles.

Left: Our favourite actor signs autographs for his adoring fans.

ight: Taylor travels all ver the world to promote s films. Here he is turning to Los Angeles ter working in Canada.

Twilight stars Taylor, Kristen and Rob arrive for the L.A. première of the latest *Twilight* film, *Eclipse*.

E is for...

Eclipse

Robert Pattinson's favourite book might be *New Moon* but for Taylor *Eclipse* beats it hands down. He loves Stephenie Meyer's third book in the *Twilight Saga* and was so excited to film it.

Taylor, Kristen and Rob revealed how they felt to Yahoo Movies. Taylor said: 'The thing is with *Eclipse*, my character has a lot of action. *Eclipse* is my favourite book.'

Kristen added: 'Bella in *New Moon* is absolutely lying to herself – she keeps telling Jacob that she's not in love with him. In *Eclipse*, she's sort of acknowledging that she is absolutely in love with Jacob and considering that her

Taylor and Kristen take questions from fans prior to the release of *Twilight: Eclipse*.

boyfriend is mortal enemies with him and there's like a battle, it's a big deal. There's all this new stuff.'

Taylor continued: 'It's perfect because *Twilight* develops Edward and Bella's relationship, *New Moon* develops Jacob's and Bella's, and the three of them are physically together in *Eclipse* – which is really, really funny because these two guys hate each other; mortal enemies who are forced to join forces to protect the girl they love. My favourite scene of the entire franchise – the entire series – is the tent scene, so to film that scene was great.'

Taylor loves the fact that Edward has to let Bella and Jacob cuddle up together in the sleeping bag because he has no choice and Bella would die if she didn't. Taylor wanted fans to enjoy the scene as much as he, Rob and Kristen enjoyed shooting it. He says there was a lot of ribbing between Edward and Jacob in the scene and the way that David Slade chose to shoot it was great too – he thinks David is incredible at visualisation.

Taylor told *Rolling Stone* magazine: 'That tent scene is the biggest thing possible. She's cold and I'm hot, so [since vampires are cold] are you going to let me crawl in the sleeping bag with her, or are you just going to let her die?'

Edi Gathegi

The actor who plays the vampire Laurent in *Twilight* and *New Moon* is Edi Gathegi. Sadly, he would only appear in two of the movies because he is killed by the wolf pack in *New Moon*.

Edi was one of Taylor's closest friends on set, so it must have been sad, turning up to filming *Eclipse* without him being there. The two of them had so much fun promoting *Twilight* together – often they were paired up and sent to different cities to the rest of the cast. During a *Twilight* Pre-Screening at Hoyts Cinema Broadway, Edi and Taylor ended up serenading Nikki Reed with their own unique version of Miley Cyrus's 'See You Again'. It's really funny and well worth a watch on YouTube. During the *Twilight* promotional tour, Edi and Taylor would do interviews together and then head to the gym every day.

Back then, Edi revealed to a journalist: 'He does not let up. I ask, "What do we do?" [and he replies] "Everything! The whole routine." I could say that he's definitely one of the most committed people that I have ever seen at the gym. I think I might have been like him when I was younger – I go off and on, even right now. This kid just stays at the focus point.

'[Taylor] does free-weights: bi's, tri's, shoulders, legs – he's ready. His job depends on it, and he has to be this way and get bigger for the rest of the series. I mean, this kid is incredible!'

Even when Taylor was told that he would be playing Jacob in *New Moon*, he still hit the gym after his family's celebration meal with Edi.

Extreme Martial Arts

Had Taylor missed the competition when Mike Chat was in the audience then he might never have been spotted and most probably would have continued with traditional martial arts. He wouldn't have been introduced to extreme martial arts and so might not

Edi Gathegi plays Laurent in *Twilight* and *New Moon*.

have had the unique skills that he could transfer to the big screen.

When Mike became Taylor's martial arts instructor, Taylor was doing extreme martial arts for the very first time. Taylor explained what happened to kidzworld.com: 'He taught me this extreme martial arts stuff and I started liking that a lot more. Regular martial arts is traditional, with no music and no flips choreographed into it, but extreme martial arts is choreographed to music: it's very fast-beat, up-tempo and you put a lot of acrobatic maneuvers into the routine.'

Taylor also revealed what his favourite martial arts trick is: 'It's called a corkscrew. It's a backflip off one leg and then you do a 360 in the air and I land it in the splits. I was the first competitor to ever land that in the National Karate Circuit.'

Wow, that sounds painful!

OPPOSITE: TAYLOR LEAVES A TV STUDIO AFTER RECORDING AN INTERVIEW IN THE RUN UP TO THE RELEASE OF *TWILIGHT: ECLIPSE*.

F is for...

Fame

The first time Taylor realised that he was famous was when some kids in a burger bar recognised him as Sharkboy, back in 1995.

He told journalist Jason Whyte: 'We've been at In-N-Out Burger and a little kid went, "Hey, it's Sharkboy, Dad! Sharkboy's over there!" We were just in an Old Navy, and they have these Sharkboy and Lavagirl T-shirts that they're selling, and one kid kept staring at me and the sticker pack that he just received with my picture on it! That was really funny, having the kid go, "Oh my gosh! You're the *real* Sharkboy! One sec, I have to go tell my friend," and he runs over, grabs him and we talk for a few minutes.'

Taylor might be one of the most famous and in-demand males on the planet, but he's never going to get big-headed. He claims his parents would never allow him to, and he's been brought up to be better than that. Dan Lautner told Terri Finch Hamilton from *The Grand Rapids Press*: 'Because of all that's happening for him, we want him to do normal things. We kept him in public school as long as we could, so he could be with his peers. We give him responsibilities at home – chores he has to do. He gets an allotted allowance and he has to budget it. We're trying to teach him things, so that when he goes out on his own, he'll be prepared.'

It's really good that Dan and Deborah Lautner have raised Taylor so he can deal with fame. There's no chance of him going off the rails like some young celebrities do, drinking heavily or becoming a complete party animal – Taylor is way too sensible to mess up his life like they do. He still likes to have fun though!

When Taylor was cast as Jacob Black, it caused his fan base to multiply by many thousands overnight. Today he has more fans than many actors who have been making blockbuster movies for decades.

Even before *Twilight* hit cinemas, Taylor was getting a lot of attention. His dad said at the time: 'It's been a crazy couple of months for the whole family – we want to protect him, we had no idea what was gonna happen. We tell him, "You have no idea what's gonna happen tomorrow, so enjoy today. Have fun.'"

Now Taylor is mega-famous you can buy almost anything with his face on it: T-shirts, mugs, duvet covers, even thongs!

Taylor talked to Fred Topel from CanMag about how it feels to be caught up in the fame game: 'I'm not online crazy 24-7, but I run across things sometimes. It's weird – it's weird to see shirts that say "Team Taylor" on them and other materials of clothing. I don't actually [have a Taylor

TAYLOR IS MOBBED BY FANS EVERYWHERE HE GOES.

thong], I'm actually not wearing it now. Definitely it's very surprising, but at the same time it's not because the fans behind it are just extraordinary. The fans are driving this thing and the storyline's awesome. [*Twilight's*] got everything in it, so it's going to be interesting to see on the big screen.'

Taylor might never have had his face on thongs before, but he did have his own action figures when he played Sharkboy. They were available in McDonald's and Target stores. Taylor must have found it quite strange to see young children playing with mini-versions of him. He kept a few *Sharkboy* figures and stored them away because he didn't have any idea that his career would blossom a few years later – he thought Sharkboy might end up being his biggest part and so he wanted to keep them as souvenirs.

Being famous does have its downside, though: Taylor can't go anywhere without being followed by paparazzi photographers. They are desperate for photos of him to sell to newspapers and media outlets. He told *Teen Vogue*: 'There are 12 cars that camp outside my house. You can't ever really get used to it, because it's not normal to have people snapping pictures of everything you do – you just have to try not to let it affect you.'

He might have millions of fans, but Taylor doesn't feel any different. He insists that he's still the same person that he was before, but he's now in a new – *Twilight* – world. Taylor told

VIP Access: 'I don't think there is anyway to prepare for it [fame]. It was weird because when we were filming *Twilight* none of us expected anything at all. We thought we were making a film for the fans to enjoy, that we were passionate about. We had no idea that this was going to happen, so it's just been an amazing experience. I'm so thankful to have been a part of it.'

Even though he has lost the opportunity to go unnoticed in a shopping centre or football game, Taylor remains optimistic and sees fame as a blessing, not a curse. He divulged to ESPN: '[Being famous is] great because it allows me to do what I want to do. It allows me to make movies, to meet and work with new people and travel the world. I'm doing what I love to do, so it's great. It's a little different with this [*Twilight*] franchise, and we have very passionate fans and the weirdest thing is none of us expected it so we're continually surprised – over and over again, everywhere we go.'

Family

Taylor was born on 11 February 1992. As she cradled him in her arms for the very first time, his mum, Deborah, was so happy. His dad, Daniel, was over the moon too as he introduced little Taylor Daniel to his grandparents and other relatives. He was their first child. It's not known how much he weighed or what time of day he was born because his family has chosen to keep this private.

But Taylor's not the only famous face to have been born on 11 February. He shares his birthday with *Destiny's Child's* Kelly Rowland and *Slipknot* star, Craig Jones (Spike-Head).

Daniel Lautner spent quite a bit of time away from his family when Taylor was younger because he was an airline pilot and had to travel far away. His mum was employed by an office design company but didn't work full time so she could spend time with Taylor. When she wasn't looking after him, Deborah enrolled him in a great little nursery.

At the age of six-and-a-half, Taylor became a big brother when his sister Makena was born. During the promotional tour of *The Adventures of Sharkboy and Lavagirl 3-D*, he explained to Michael J. Lee from RadioFree: 'My sister and I would always be spies when I was younger. We'd be in the house, and I'd hide something, and I'd act like we were secret agents and spies. And I'd tell her that it was really happening, and she still believes me to this day. She's six. [Laughs] Pretty soon, I gotta tell her that it's just fake and I'm trying to make her have fun!'

Taylor has remained really close to his sister, even though he has to spend time away from her when he is filming. There are no jealousy issues at all between the

TAYLOR GOT INTO ACTING THROUGH HIS MARTIAL ARTS TUTOR, MIKE CHAT.

two of them. When *Seventeen* magazine asked Robert Pattinson which member of his family he was closest to, he picked his dog Patty. For Taylor, no thinking was required – he simply chose his sister Makena.

He said: 'My sister, because she looks up to me but I also look up to her in a way. She's younger – she's only 10 – so I'm probably going to be one of those brothers who are watching her with boys, which she's probably not going to like too much.'

Makena and Taylor actually look scarily alike and often hang out together. They even share friends and Makena has recently been photographed out shopping with Taylor's close friend, Selena Gomez. Both Taylor and Makena have dark skin, but Taylor admits that he doesn't know why this is. He confessed to *MediaBlvd* magazine: 'I'm mostly French, Dutch and German. I'm not really sure where I get the dark, tan skin from – it just kind of happened.'

Fans

Taylor loves his fans so much. He thinks they're the best fans anyone could ever have. Some of his fans have been following his career since 2005, when he was only 13. He showed so much potential in *The Adventure of Sharkboy and Lavagirl 3-D* that they just knew that one day he'd be a massive star. How right they were!

Taylor's first fans were even younger than he was: they saw him as the real-life Sharkboy rather than Taylor Lautner. Taylor didn't mind, though – he just liked meeting the fans and making them happy.

He admitted to journalist Terri Finch Hamilton: '10-year-old boys were the ones who first recognised me. I'd be in the store and boys would whisper to their moms. Then the moms would say, "Excuse me – are you Sharkboy?" I just thought it was so cool – I couldn't believe people wanted my picture!'

At first, Taylor's fans were mainly boys but after he scored the part of Eliot Murtaugh in *Cheaper by the Dozen 2*, he started getting female fans. Girls began to go crazy when they caught a glimpse of him because of his good looks rather than the martial arts skills that the boys rated from *Sharkboy*.

Taylor didn't realise it, but as soon as it was announced that he would be playing the part of Jacob Black he gained many more fans, even though they hadn't actually seen *Twilight* yet. A naïve Taylor thought it might be a good idea to head on down to his local bookstore when *Breaking Dawn* was released. Stephenie Meyer's fourth *Twilight* book was launched in over 4,000 stores at midnight on 2 August 2008 and sold 1.3 million copies in the first 24 hours!

Poor Taylor had no idea what was going to happen that night. As soon as he entered the bookstore, some *Twilight* fans spotted him. He told *The Grand Rapids Press*: 'They shouted: "That's Jacob Black! It's Jacob Black!" Then I heard this mom say, "No, that kid's name is Taylor – he used to live across the street from me." And the girls said, "No, that's Jacob Black." And the mom said, "No, that's Taylor – he's my old neighbor." She didn't know I was gonna be in the movie.'

He ended up staying signing autographs for two hours: 'I didn't realize 1,000 girls were gonna be there! I would feel miserable if I left and there were still 100 girls who had been waiting two hours to get my autograph.'

Taylor always wants to thank the loyal fans that queue up for hours just to catch a glimpse of him as he goes into TV studios or awards shows. He finds it difficult when he has to rush from place to place, so he can't spend all that much time with them. Some fans aren't happy with Taylor signing a piece of paper, a book or a photograph: they want him to sign their underwear!

Taylor told movies.about.com about his weirdest fan encounter: 'There was some middle-aged woman. She's like, "Guess what, Taylor? I'm wearing the Team Taylor panties!" I'm like, "No way!" And she's like, "Would you mind signing them?" And luckily my publicist was right there and she's like, "We've got to go do an interview." And I'm like, "Okay, yeah, I'll think about that one."'

It's a good job Taylor's publicist rescued him – he never likes to disappoint his fans and so it would

TAYLOR POSES FOR A PICTURE WITH ONE OF HIS MANY FANS.

have been horrible if he had felt like he had to sign those panties!

Taylor, Kristen and Rob all love their individual fans and fans of the *Twilight* movies in general. They have always wanted to make great movies that the fans will love. Sometimes this can add a lot of pressure to their young shoulders. When *Twilight* was being filmed, they had only a tiny idea of what the fans wanted, but with *New Moon* they knew that the pressure was on to make an even better film.

Taylor confessed to Rebecca Murray from

Movies.About.com: 'Sometimes it can be nerve-racking. It's hard not to be nervous when you know there's a few million fans out there who are just dying for this movie to come out and making sure it's top-notch, the best and the characters are wonderful. So I mean, yes, it gets nerve-racking sometimes but for the most part, I'm just really excited. I'm totally stoked to be a part of it!'

Taylor's fans come in all shapes and sizes, the only thing they have in common is that they all love Taylor. You can be 5-years-old or even 75, it really doesn't matter. Some fans faint when they see Taylor, others stop breathing and have to be given first aid. It really is crazy!

It doesn't seem to have hit Taylor yet that the fans are more into *him* than his character, Jacob Black. It's Taylor's name that they shout on the red carpet, not Jacob's. Taylor has so many fans around the world that he's really not sure which country has the best fans. He admitted on the *Lopez Tonight Show*: 'Brazil was really intense – the fans were really aggressive there, but it's a good thing. There were a few fun incidents in Brazil. We were in Munich and we were at a stadium full of 25,000 girls and when you walk out, you can't hear anything – you walk out and it takes a good half-hour to get a little bit of your hearing back.'

Taylor's fans in Brazil were so intense that a bunch of them stormed the hotel where Taylor and Kristen Stewart were staying in. Taylor had to stay in his room while riot police secured the building: 'All of a sudden, Security comes up to the room and they say, "Hey, so 2,000 fans just broke into the hotel and the police with riot gear are trying to keep them out of this room."

'We're like, "What do we do? What?"'

This incident would have probably scared most people, but Taylor seems to have taken it all in his stride. He is forever telling people how great and talented his fans are and he loves the scrapbooks that his fans make him and the DVDs they put together with clips and music. Taylor really appreciates all the hard work that they put in to give him personal gifts.

He doesn't even mind when fans follow him into restaurant toilets. He says that normally, they wait outside until he's finished and then ask him for an autograph or photo. Some people find this a bit creepy, but Taylor understands that they just want to see him. Fans of Robert Pattinson do the same but more often than not, they wait outside restaurants where they know the *Twilight* stars are dining because they know that Rob will need to pop outside for a cigarette break or two and they can corner him then!

Film Making

Taylor might be famous for his acting skills now, but he was quite a talented amateur director when he was younger. While other kids played hide-n-seek and tag, he preferred to shoot movies with his Lavagirl friend, Taylor Dooley.

A 12-year-old Taylor told eFilmCritic: 'I make movies with my sister, Taylor Dooley, and her brother all the time. We're making one right now with my video camera and my stills camera, and it's a lot of fun. We have credits and music that we edit on the computer. The one we're doing now is called *Ladynappers* and it stars Taylor's brother as the Ladynapper, and he kidnaps Jamie – who Taylor Dooley plays – and he takes her away in downtown New York City.

'I play a CIA Secret Agent, who has to go on an adventure to find Jamie and bring her back and capture the Ladynapper, and on my way I find difficulties because it's downtown New York. And I find Goth Girl, played by my sister, who lives on the streets and therefore knows all of the town's secrets. It's a group of action and comedy, and it's just a lot of fun to make [laughs]. We were making one like that when we were down in Austin, Texas, filming *Sharkboy* and Robert Rodriguez's wife Elizabeth told us that if we could finish it, maybe we could put it on the DVD, but we never finished it [laughs].'

Taylor sounded so enthusiastic about *Ladynappers* that it's a shame it's never been seen in public. It must have taken them ages to write the script and plan what was going to happen. Taylor must have the potential to become a great film producer or director one day. Lots of amazing actors do both – Russell Crowe, Tom Cruise and Mel Gibson have all produced and directed their own movies. Adam Sandler has been a writer and producer on several film projects, too.

Fire

Not many people know this, but Taylor is lucky to be alive. When he was four years old, there was a huge fire at his home and his family lost all their possessions as their house was completely gutted. Luckily, Taylor and his mum were staying at his aunt's house at the time – if they had been home, they would almost certainly have died.

Taylor's dad was working away then and so his aunt asked Deborah if she wanted to pop over with Taylor instead of being in an empty house.

Taylor admitted to his local paper, *The Grand Rapids Press*: 'The police called and told us our house had burned down. If my aunt hadn't invited us to sleep over… well, wow!'

Food

Taylor has always loved food, but he has never been greedy. His active lifestyle means that he has to eat good, healthy food. He used to love eating chocolate and sweets when he was younger, though, as a special treat.

In fact, one of Taylor's favourite scenes in *The Adventures of Sharkboy and Lavagirl 3-D* involved eating a lot of food. He told *Ultimatedisney.com* all about it: 'We're on the giant cookie and I got to step in a big puddle of chocolate and then I got to eat it. And I also liked getting whipped cream and ice cream all over us...that was fun. It was real chocolate and then the ice cream was actually just colored whipped cream. Because we land on the cake and there's supposed to be frosting and ice cream and we got whipped cream on us. I also liked my scene where I sing and I fight with the plugs. Those were probably my favorite couple of scenes.'

Taylor might have always eaten healthily but he had to step it up another level as soon as *Twilight* wrapped. He had a limited time to get his body to the level required to play Jacob Black in *New Moon* and so he enlisted professional help to make sure that his diet and fitness regime was both effective and safe. Most people might think that it would be the exercise that would be the toughest thing for Taylor to adapt to, but he insists that it

Taylor's *My Own Worst Enemy* co-star, Christian Slater

was his change in diet that required the most work. He had to avoid going to the ice cream parlour and instead had to stay at home and eat a lot of meat.

Going to the gym didn't stress Taylor out because he knew that if he wanted to play Jacob, then he had to put in the hours. Eating all the right things, all the time was tough, however. Every two hours without fail, he had to eat meat patties, sweet potatoes and raw almonds. He also had to drink protein shakes that tasted truly disgusting.

Co-star Kristen Stewart was really impressed with the way that Taylor handled his change in diet. Before, he had stuck to the same type of meals all the time – for instance, he'd never even tried sushi before she suggested it. He was just used to the food that his mum always cooked him.

The average man needs about 2,500 calories a day but Taylor needed to take in more because of all the exercise he was going to be doing. He revealed to iesb.com: 'I found out that I had to consume at least 3,200 calories a day just to maintain, and I was trying to gain, so I had to eat more than that. And I had to put something in my mouth every two hours. I'm busy – I'd be in downtown L.A., going from meeting to meeting, and there was not time for me to be eating. So, I literally would have to carry a little baggie of beef patties, raw almonds and sweet potatoes. It was difficult.'

Poor Taylor! He'll have to stay away from ice cream and cakes for quite a few years yet because after the *Twilight*

Saga movies finish, no doubt he'll be doing more action movies so he'll need to keep looking buff. It might be tough for him, but it'll be worth it if he becomes the new Bruce Willis!

Football

Robert Pattinson's passion might be music and writing, but for Taylor, it's American football that floats his boat. He just can't get enough of it.

Taylor confessed to *Aced* magazine: 'My character's special thing is mechanics, but for me, I guess it would be football. I played football my whole life and had to give it up last year because I had to miss too many practices and it was kind of rough for me. It is kind of hard watching the high-school football games now. I played running back and slot receiver and strong safety on defense.'

He might not play for a team any more, but he still likes messing around with his mates on set. Robert Pattinson may be rubbish at sports, but Kristen Stewart is actually rather good. Taylor thinks she has lots of potential as she is great at throwing the ball accurately and can catch too. At first he just used to play with the lads on set, but now he lets Kristen join in too and she has become his 'American football buddy'.

When he has any spare time (which isn't very often),

our favourite actor loves watching college teams play. During the promotional tour for *The Adventures of Sharkboy and Lavagirl 3-D*, he talked to Mark Sells from *The Reel Deal* about his favourite teams. Back then, he said: 'My favorite college team is the Michigan Wolverines because I was born and raised in Michigan. And they're actually pretty good, too! As for NFL [National Football League], I don't really have a favorite. I like the Atlanta Falcons because I think Michael Vick is really, really good. And I like the Philadelphia Eagles. But I'm a big college fan — we watch college football a lot.

'We try to be Detroit fans, but it's really tough. We are, however, big Detroit Pistons fans — who were champions last year and are in the finals this year. And I can't wait to watch them play the Spurs!'

No one can really blame Taylor for struggling to support the Detroit Lions Football team. In 1998, they became the only team in NFL history to lose all 16 of their regular season games. Things improved slightly in September 2009 when they managed to beat the Washington Redskins 19–14, after a 19-game losing streak.

It's not known if Taylor still supports the same teams or if he has switched his allegiances: it's been a few years and often young boys change the teams that they support as they grow up and their favourite players switch teams or retire. Taylor has been photographed with his dad at an

LA Lakers game against the San Antonio Spurs and it's thought that he was cheering on the LA Lakers. Taylor wasn't the only celebrity in the audience, either: Kim and Khloe Kardashian were also there and Eva Longoria-Parker was cheering on her hubby Tony, who plays for the San Antonio Spurs.

Friends

Taylor's best friends might be the friends that he had when he was just a kid, but he still considers the people that he has worked with to be good mates.

In November 2008, he told Adrienne Gaffney from *Vanity Fair*: 'The [*Twilight*] cast really had great chemistry and we all hung out. We're all really good friends now, so that's really cool.'

Taylor was actually the youngest member of the *Twilight* cast for the first two movies. It was tough in the beginning because he didn't know if they would accept him as an equal or just treat him as a kid. He admits: 'I was a little nervous at first but no, it was great. I can't even tell the difference. Everybody's really nice and easy to relate to.'

It's great that Taylor gelled with the other cast members straight away. After all, he is 6 years younger than Robert Pattinson, 13 years younger than Edi Gathegi (Laurent) and

TAYLOR GOT ON REALLY WELL WITH ALL THE CAST MEMBERS OF THE *TWILIGHT SAGA*, INCLUDING PETER FACINELLI WHO PLAYS CARLISLE CULLEN.

19 years younger that Peter Facinelli (Carlisle). It must have been nice for him when BooBoo Stewart joined the cast for *Eclipse* because he is two years younger.

While filming *New Moon* and *Eclipse*, Taylor and the rest of the cast spent lots of nights hanging out together in Vancouver restaurants and bars. Whenever Jackson Rathbone (Jasper Hale in *Twilight*) was performing with his band 100 Monkeys, they would head for his gigs to show their support.

When Taylor was asked by iesb.com in an interview which cast member he was closest to, he couldn't decide. He said: 'I wouldn't be able to pick one. If I were to start, I'd end up listing the whole cast. I do spend a lot of time with Kristen because all my scenes are involved with her, so Kristen and I are very close. I guess I'm close with Rob, too, because we spend a lot of time together as well. But the great thing about this series is that the whole entire cast is so close and it would be a nightmare if we weren't. It would be impossible to make this series because the characters are so tight, so we're really thankful that we all get along so well.'

Fun Facts

Favourite movie? *Iron Man*.

Favourite TV shows? *American Idol* and *So You Think You Can Dance*.

Favourite band? Black Eyed Peas.

Dream car? Ferrari Enzo.

Secret talent? Drawing.

Dream actors to work with? Denzel Washington, Matt Damon or Mark Wahlberg.

Celebrity crush? It was Jessica Alba, but it's now Megan Fox.

Eyes? Hazel-brown.

Favourite breakfast cereal? Reese's Puffs.

Most prized possession? His Warrior Cup trophy from martial arts days.

Favourite date meal? Pizza.

Favourite food? Steak or Chinese.

Pets? Taylor loves dogs and he has a Maltese called Roxy.

MEGAN FOX,
TAYLOR'S SECRET
CELEBRITY CRUSH.

G is for...

Gil Birmingham

The actor who plays Billy Black in the *Twilight Saga* movies is Gil Birmingham. He has been acting professionally since 1986 and has been in many TV shows and movies. Gil is of Comanche (Native American) ancestry and is best known for his roles in the movies *End of the Spear* and *DreamKeeper*.

Gil really enjoys playing Taylor's on-screen dad and told Twilight Lexicon: 'Billy Burke is such an open personality that playing best friends just came naturally. And Taylor is the kind of young man that any father would be proud to have as a son. I feel as strongly about Kristen Stewart and

GIL BIRMINGHAM PLAYS BILLY BLACK IN THE *TWILIGHT SAGA*.

Robert Pattinson – they are all wonderful and talented people. Good times!'

Gil and Taylor hit it off straight away and during the audition process, proved to Catherine Hardwicke that they had great chemistry. As Gil explained: 'Catherine Hardwicke paired me up with different actors auditioning for the role of Jacob, my son. At first we were asked to read the scripted lines and then we did considerably more improvisation scenes. It's really about the look *and* the chemistry – it's nice when you audition and capture moments of magic.'

Now that Taylor has a wolf pack, Gil likes to nickname them the 'Puppy Pack' because the rest of the cast can be calmly reading a scene when Taylor, Chaske and the rest of the boys rush in, all excited and full of energy. It seems they can change the mood on set in an instant, just like hyperactive puppies!

Girlfriends

It's amazing that a guy as sexy as Taylor can be single. He could have practically any girl he wanted as his girlfriend because he's so popular right now, but instead he remains unattached.

In the past, Taylor has said that he isn't allowed to date until he is 28 years old, but hopefully his parents may have

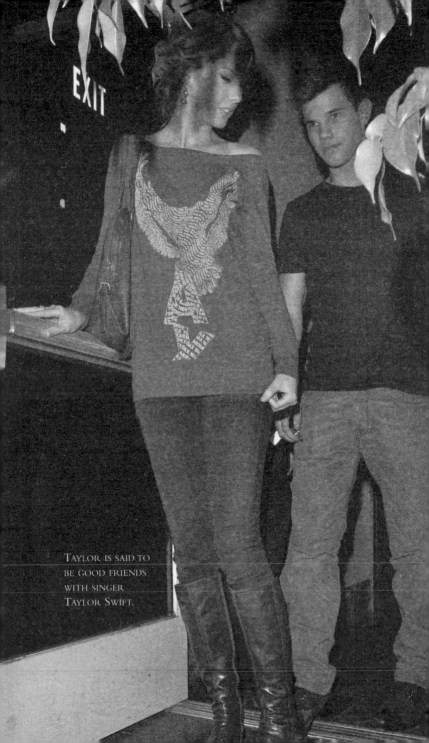

TAYLOR IS SAID TO
BE GOOD FRIENDS
WITH SINGER
TAYLOR SWIFT.

relaxed that rule! If you think you could be the perfect girl for Taylor, you might like to know what sort of girl he is looking for.

Taylor's ideal girl would be someone who is comfortable in their own skin and happy to let the world see who she really is. He doesn't want to date someone who is false or just pretending to be someone she isn't. For instance, he would hate it if a girl pretended to be passionate about football only for her to turn round later and say she hates it and that she only said she liked it to make him like her. Taylor would also like it if the girl was confident enough to approach him – sometimes he is too shy to do all the chasing himself. He really wishes that he could feel relaxed and open all the time because this is how he would like his ideal girl to be, but sometimes he struggles with letting his guard down.

Taylor talked to *Seventeen* magazine about what he considers to be a relationship deal-breaker: 'If a girl doesn't know how to smile or laugh, or if they try to play cool all the time. Playing hard to get is not the way to win me over. I'm definitely more for the girl who can smile and laugh all the time and just have a good time!'

All of Taylor's fans would love to see Taylor settle down one day with his perfect girl. He deserves to have that special person who loves him no matter what. It would be nice for Taylor if there was someone waiting for him every night when he came back from shooting his scenes, but at the end of the day he is still only a teenager and so he needs to be free to do what he wants. If he wants to go play footy with his friends, he should be able to do this without thinking that he has to be somewhere else. Lots of Taylor's fans dream about being his girlfriend one day.

H is for...

Hair

Lots of the actors and actresses in the *Twilight* cast have had to change their hairstyles to play their roles. Stephenie Meyer described her characters' hairstyles very specifically in the *Twilight Saga* books so in order to be true to the books, several of the actors had to wear wigs. Taylor was one of the unlucky ones and he found wearing a wig really uncomfortable. Wearing Jacob's clothes were easy, but wearing the wig was tough because it took so long to put on and take off!

In an ideal world, Taylor would have grown his natural hair for the part rather than wear a wig, but this would have been impossible as it could take years to grow his hair so long. He told Rebecca Murray from Movies.About.com: 'It definitely would be more comfortable [having naturally long hair rather than a wig]. I just don't think I could stand walking around like that in public. I don't know, it's so weird looking at myself in the mirror and going, "Is that me?" It's like, it looks so different – it's weird to me. It's like, "Wow!" I've never had my hair longer than it is right now, so just looking at myself…is like, "Wow, do I look like a girl? I do look like a girl, argh!"'

Wearing the wig was painful because it was glued to his head and made his scalp itchy; it also got in the way when he was filming. Taylor found it frustrating when he was filming intense scenes with Bella and suddenly a piece of hair would fly in his mouth and ruin the shot. Then they'd have to start again from the beginning, even if it was getting late and everyone was tired.

When Jacob transforms in *New Moon* he gets much shorter hair, which Taylor was thrilled about. He was so excited about losing the wig! When he filmed his last, long-haired scene, the crew clapped and cheered; they asked Taylor if he would like to keep the wig as a memento but he wasn't keen. He told them that if they gave it back to him, he would burn it!

Opposite: Taylor likes to keep his hair short and neat.

He's a Bully, Charlie Brown

In 2006, Taylor's voice was used in the cartoon *He's a Bully, Charlie Brown*. His role was the bully who greets Charlie Brown and Snoopy when they arrive at summer camp. Taylor's character is horrible to Charlie Brown, but when he makes a sly dig at Snoopy for bringing a bowling ball, he gets a lot more than he bargained for. Snoopy drops it on his foot to teach him a lesson.

Taylor's character wasn't in any more episodes but it was still a great show to add to his impressive CV.

Home

Taylor's parents were living in Grand Rapids, Michigan, when he was born. Grand Rapids is the largest city in Kent County and West Michigan. It sits on the Grand River and is approximately 30 miles from Lake Michigan. Grand Rapids is a very beautiful place and there are lots of things to do – it's got a massive zoo, several museums, lovely beaches and places to go skiing and snowmobiling. You could never get bored on a trip to Grand Rapids.

Taylor's first home was on Rosewood Avenue, Grand Rapids. It wasn't the biggest house in the world, but it was on a nice street and there were plenty of parks and good schools for Taylor to go to when he was old enough.

In 1996, his parents decided to move 20 miles away to a bigger house in Hudsonville. This home was a lot closer to Taylor's aunties and uncles. They must have thought that it would be nicer for four-year-old Taylor to grow up alongside his cousins and wider family. Shortly after they made the move Deborah found out that she was expecting her second baby. When Makena was born, Taylor couldn't have been happier: he dotes on his little sister.

Hudsonville is a much smaller city than Grand Rapids. It only has about 7,160 residents compared to approximately 197,800 who live in Grand Rapids. Taylor and his family were really happy living in Hudsonville. He went to a great school called Jamestown Elementary School and they had loads of friends in the city. When Taylor started acting, they didn't realise how much it would impact on their home life. Because auditions were taking place in Los Angeles, they couldn't keep travelling all the time and so they had to move or Taylor would have to give up acting.

Taylor admitted to *The Reel Deal*: 'It was a very, very hard decision. Our family and friends did not want us to go, but our choices were: we could stay in Michigan and I could give up acting (I would have had to because it would have been crazy to continually fly out from

Michigan to California each time there was an audition!), or we could move to California and I could continue to act. I told my parents I didn't want to give up acting. And after weighing the good with bad, they agreed to move.'

Taylor might be living in Los Angeles now, but his heart will always be where he used to live in Michigan – he loves making the long journey back to see his family and friends. He told Terri Finch Hamilton from *The Grand Rapids Press*: 'I love coming back here. In LA, whatever you do for fun, you gotta spend money. Here, you go jet skiing on a lake. It's such a fun place for me: I go fishing with one set of grandparents, I go quadriding with the other set; we go trap shooting – it's so much fun. Here, people are way more down-to-earth.'

Maybe in the future Taylor might buy a house in LA and another one in Michigan, near his grandparents, so he can stay there when he's not shooting movies.

Hope For Haiti Now

On Tuesday, 12 January 2010 there was a massive earthquake in Haiti and in the two weeks that followed, 52 more aftershocks were experienced. Millions of people around the world started to donate money and pray for those trapped under the rubble and left behind.

George Clooney decided that he needed to do

something big to help and rallied as many celebrities as possible to perform in a TV fundraising event called 'Hope For Haiti Now'. Justin Timberlake, Bono, Coldplay and Beyoncé all performed, as well as a whole host of other big names. Taylor wanted to get involved and so he manned the phone lines with Zac Efron, Vanessa Hudgens, Selena Gomez and the Jonas Brothers. Other stars such as Robert Pattinson voiced direct appeals to the people at home watching, pleading with them to pick up their phones and donate to the worthy cause.

TAYLOR AND THE JONAS BROTHERS TOOK PHONE CALLS DURING THE *HOPE FOR HAITI* CAMPAIGN.

The songs performed were also available on iTunes, with all the proceeds going to the appeal fund.

The $57 million raised by the Hope For Haiti Now concert and TV event went to the Red Cross, Unicef, Oxfam America, Partners in Health and Wyclef Jean's Yéle Haiti Foundation.

It's great that Taylor supported such a worthwhile cause and did what he could to convince his fans to donate to the Hope For Haiti Now fund.

I is for...

Internet

The Internet is a great tool for Taylor's fans to keep in touch with him and with each other. They share photos and stories about Taylor and if anyone spots him out and about, they can let the other fans know where he is. There are some great Taylor Lautner fan sites on the net that are well worth checking out.

If you go on Twitter and Facebook don't be fooled into thinking that profiles set up in Taylor's name are actually your favourite actor. Taylor has no profiles on social networking sites. He does, however, have his own website.

A few years ago, when he started getting TV and

film roles Taylor set up his own website – www.taylorlautner.com – so that he could keep in touch with his fans. He liked to post up messages and photos for them to look at and also had a contact page so they could write to him and ask him questions. He would also send them an autograph, if they asked for one. Back then, Taylor was thrilled when his website got 20 hits a day and was flabbergasted when he received 3,000 in a month shortly before *The Adventures of Sharkboy and Lavagirl 3-D* came out.

Sadly, his website isn't working at the moment, but hopefully he will get it up and running again soon. He might have got a couple of hundred hits a month in the past, but those days are long gone. Now he'll easily get millions of hits a month as every Taylor fan would check it out several times a day, if they could.

Taylor does occasionally check out what people write about him on the Internet when he has some free time, but he doesn't Google his name or anything. He knows that magazines and websites can make up stories to get people to read them and so he doesn't take things to heart; he likes checking out *Twilight* fan sites and seeing how passionate and dedicated the fans are.

Many people think that Robert Pattinson is the most popular actor in the *Twilight Saga* movies, but they are wrong. According to a recent study by CNN, Taylor is more popular by quite a large margin with kids in their search engine histories than Robert. Taylor came 80th in the CNN study's top 100 list of kids' search terms – Robert Pattinson didn't even make the top 100.

Taylor doesn't just read news sites and fan sites when he is on the Internet. He also likes to go on computer games websites. He told *Seventeen* magazine: 'I'm not on the computer that much, but I used to go to this website called addictinggames.com. It has the coolest games and a lot of variety, so whenever I was bored, I would just go on that.'

Taylor does get a little bit freaked out if fans send him weird links. He explained to *Vanity Fair*: 'One of the other weirdest fan things is somebody sent me a link and said, "What is this?" And it was a picture of women's underwear being sold online with "Taylor" written on it, so it was kind of weird to have women's underwear with my name imprinted on the front.'

If you love Taylor, there are quite a few cool websites dedicated to him where you can find the latest gossip, plus more general *Twilight* websites that cover all the main stars. Here are five of the best websites for you to check out:

www.stepheniemeyer.com – Stephenie Meyer's official website.
www.twilightlexicon.com – A site for everything *Twilight*.

www.twilightguide.com – A great site for the latest filming gossip and interviews with the cast.

www.taylorlautner.org – This site is updated several times a day with the latest Taylor news.

www.lautnerfan.com – If you want the latest photos of Taylor, then you need to head over to lautnerfan.com.

J is for...

Jackson Rathbone

The talented actor and musician who plays Jasper Hale in the *Twilight Saga* movies is Jackson Rathbone. Before *Twilight*, Jackson was in several TV shows and movies, including *The O.C.*, *Beautiful People* and *The Valley of Light*. He was actually one of the actors that fans of the *Twilight* books wanted to play Edward Cullen before Robert Pattinson was cast.

Jackson admires the way that Taylor has worked hard to get his body in shape but believes that his eyes are the feature that draws in the fans when they watch *New Moon*. He thinks Taylor's eyes convey lots of emotion and

TAYLOR AND HIS *TWILIGHT* CO-STAR JACKSON ARE REALLY GOOD FRIENDS.

it's by looking at Jacob and Bella's eyes in the movie that you realise that she is falling for him.

All the cast were shocked by the reaction that the *New Moon* trailer received the first time it was shown. As Jackson explained to MTV, as soon as Taylor took off his top in the trailer, they started screaming: 'You can't hear the rest of the [trailer] because it's just screams and screams. I think they were happy screams!'

Jackson really appreciates it when Taylor comes to his band's performances, even if he's had a long day filming. Often Taylor can be seen jumping up and down at the front, cheering on his friend. Usually, it's really hot and Taylor gets very sweaty, but he doesn't seem to mind. He likes the music that the 100 Monkeys perform and getting the opportunity to talk to *Twilight* fans in the crowd.

Jacob Black

Jacob Black is the character that Taylor is most famous for playing. In years to come, he will be associated with other big movie roles, but for now he is the real-life Jacob Black from *Twilight* for millions of girls worldwide.

The Jacob Black that we fall in love with in *New Moon* is actually pretty much the real Taylor Lautner. Not only do Jacob and Taylor look identical, but they share the same character traits, too and the fact that he was just like

Jacob made Taylor really want to play him. He also likes Jacob's split personality because when he is a werewolf, he is the complete opposite to how Taylor is in real life – the real Taylor could never be aggressive or territorial.

As he explained to Larry Carroll from MTV: 'Jacob Black is a Native American. He's part of the Quileute tribe. He eventually turns into a werewolf, which is really cool. I love the contrast between the Native American side of him and the werewolf. His Native American side, he is very friendly and outgoing. He loves Bella and is very loyal to Bella and his dad. But on the werewolf side, they're very fierce and just attacking, and they have this huge temper so there's a lot of stress and things going on inside him as he's trying to keep his temper to himself. I love that part, which Stephenie created, with the contrast between the Native American side and the werewolf side of him.'

Many *Twilight* fans view Edward Cullen as being the outsider but Taylor thinks that Jacob is the real outsider because he doesn't go to the same school as everyone else. If it wasn't for Bella, he wouldn't have any friends outside the reservation. He thinks Jacob is Bella's sun because he's the one who stops her feeling depressed and makes her smile again.

Taylor didn't mind having just a small role in the first *Twilight* movie because he knew that *New Moon* would concentrate on his character's relationship with Bella, rather than Edward Cullen's relationship with her. By having such a small part, Taylor was able to see how the fans went crazy for Robert Pattinson and mentally prepare himself for a similar reaction when *New Moon* came out. He must have known that many Team Edward fans would switch sides to join Team Jacob.

Filming *New Moon* meant Taylor needed to be really focused and dedicated. Overnight, he had to go from playing a clumsy kid to a sexy man/werewolf. He revealed to *Interview* magazine: 'He's a lot different than he was before. He transforms mid-story – in the first half, he's *Twilight* Jacob. I'm wearing a wig. My character's very clumsy, outgoing, and friendly. When he transforms into a werewolf, he becomes something very different. It's like I'm playing a split personality which is tricky because sometimes I've had to play pre- and post-transformation Jacob on the same day of filming.'

In Taylor's eyes, the best thing about the *Twilight Saga* movies is that they stay very true to Stephenie Meyer's books. None of the directors involved decided to ignore the books and mix things up – the Jacob Black we read about is the one we see on-screen. Taylor likes the fact that the story isn't just about love, but contains loads of action, too – so boys as well as girls can really enjoy seeing the movies. He likes the fact that there is a wolf pack and vampires.

Playing Jacob in *New Moon* and *Eclipse* was a great honour for Taylor and he loved bringing out the new werewolf side of his character, even though CGI played a big part, too.

Rotten Tomatoes journalist Jen Yamato was lucky enough to be invited to see Taylor on set and filming some of his scenes. He told her: 'I think the most important thing with Jacob is that pre-transformation, he's clumsy – he trips over his own feet. As soon as he transforms, he's very agile. At one point, he flings himself through Bella's window and lands at her feet, and that's the first time Bella realizes this is a new Jacob: he never used to be this agile. I loved bringing out that side of him. The bummer is, when he becomes a wolf, that's not actually me. When he does the cool fight scenes, he's transformed into CGI.'

CGI stands for computer-generated imagery, which is applying 3D computer graphics to special effects in films. It means that when Jacob Black transforms, it is not Taylor that we see, but a 3D computer graphic. Even when he growls, it is CGI, not Taylor. That's a real shame, but at least it makes the wolf look so realistic. Taylor still had to do all the other scenes, which saw Jacob change, physically and mentally, into a different person, though.

Though Taylor might be a bit gutted that his wolf scenes were computerised, he was pleased that they decided to use his eye. He told Access Hollywood: 'It's really cool, when you see that first time Bella makes that connection with my Jacob wolf, you see a close-up of the eye and it's actually my eye. They scanned my eye and put my eye in the wolf, so that's really cool!'

For quite a while it was thought that Summit would fire

Taylor from *New Moon* and get another actor to play Jacob Black because of how much he has to change physically from *Twilight* to *New Moon*. *Scorpion 2* star Michael Copon was the hot favourite to take over, but *Twilight* fans refused to accept that anyone other than Taylor could play the role. They bombarded Michael Copon's Facebook profile with negative messages and signed petitions demanding Taylor be given the thumbs-up by Summit and director Chris Weitz.

Taylor didn't get involved in the debate himself and instead continued with his efforts to build himself up so that he could prove to Chris that he could still handle the part and was the right person for the job. As he revealed to VIP Access: 'During that entire time, I couldn't let it get to me – I would have failed. So I left all that stuff outside, I let people say what they wanted, think what they wanted and I just stayed focused on what I could control and it all worked out for the best.'

Everyone was so relieved when it was announced that Taylor was to play Jacob in the remaining *Twilight Saga* movies after all. It just wouldn't have been right seeing someone else as Jacob Black.

Jamie Foxx

You might be wondering why the Academy Award-winning actor, singer and comedian Jamie Foxx is included in this *Taylor Lautner A–Z*. After all, Jamie is such a superstar that you could be fooled into thinking that he doesn't even know who Taylor is. You might think that he's been included because Taylor is a massive fan of Jamie Foxx, but you'd be wrong: Jamie is Taylor's biggest celebrity fan.

Taylor let the cat out of the bag on the *Lopez Tonight* show: 'It was a year ago at the *Twilight* première and we'd just shown the movie. We're walking out of the theatre and there's tons of fans – all these high-pitched voices: "Rob", "Rob", "Taylor", "Taylor" – and we're turning in every direction possible, pictures, signing autographs, and all of a sudden I hear this deep voice from behind me: "Taylor, Taylor!" And I turn around and like, that's an interesting one. And I look back and this guy walks up to me and he goes, "Hey, my daughter's a huge fan and I'm a huge fan. Is there any way I could get a picture with you? I'm Jamie Foxx." And I was like, [speechless]. I was like, "Can I get a picture with you?" It was so weird.'

Wow! Taylor must have felt like he was dreaming or something to have such an amazing actor wanting his autograph. Maybe one day they could work together. Jamie Foxx would be a great person to teach Taylor how to improve his acting skills and handle fame.

ACTOR JAMIE FOXX IS A HUGE FAN OF TAYLOR'S.

K is for...

karate

Taylor would have never become the amazing actor he is today if he hadn't taken up karate when he was six years old. It was through karate that he developed his martial arts skills and was encouraged to go to auditions for film and TV shows.

Taylor's first karate class was called Little Dragons and it was for little boys and girls aged four to six. It was held in Fabiano's Karate and Fitness Center, just a few miles away from Taylor's home. The young Taylor took to karate like a duck to water and was always excited about the new skills he was learning in the class run by Sensei Tom Fabiano.

Sensei Tom Fabiano is a very experienced karate instructor, who has been named Michigan's Karate Instructor of the Year for the last 10 years. Children at his school learn the Matsumura Seito Shorin Ryu style of karate, which is similar to the style that Mr. Miyagi teaches his prodigy Daniel in *The Karate Kid* movies. Students of Sensei Tom Fabiano are expected to keep three creeds: 'Creed 1: I intend to develop myself in a positive manner and avoid anything that would reduce my mental growth or my physical health. Creed 2: I intend to develop self-discipline in order to bring out the best in myself and others. Creed 3: I intend to use what I learn in class constructively and only for the defense of myself and my fellow man.'

Most boys get into martial arts because their father or older brothers have studied them or because their parents want them to be able to defend themselves, but that wasn't the case for Taylor. He told Kidzworld.com and karateangels.com: 'My mom's bosses' kids were doing martial arts, and since they were doing it, I just wanted to try it. So I started and it was a lot of fun, except for the part about being barefoot. I don't like being barefoot – I don't even wear sandals. I really liked class because of all the games we got to play, like "sensei says"… I didn't really care too much for the push-ups and all the hard work. I really started because of all the fun games.'

Taylor might have only been young when he started,

but Sensei Tom Fabiano could already see that he had lots of potential: he wasn't running around, messing about like some of the other children in the class, but always listened and focused on what he had been asked to do. He put in a lot of time and effort to make sure that he mastered every move.

Many years might have passed since Taylor was under the instruction of Sensei Tom Fabiano, but he hasn't forgotten his old karate teacher or the school where he started learning martial arts. Whenever he is in the area, he pops back and says hello. Sensei Tom Fabiano told his local paper, the *Grand Rapids Press*: 'He signs autographs for all the kids, poses for pictures. He's still that well-mannered, great kid. There was one mom here, a big *Twilight* fan, and when I told her Taylor was gonna stop in, she screamed, "I *have* to meet him!"'

Kellan Lutz

Emmett Cullen in the *Twilight Saga* movies is played by Kellan Lutz: he might be playing one of Jacob's enemies but in real life he gets on really well with Taylor. They are both sports mad and enjoy working out. The two have been snapped together flying from LA to Vancouver and hang out at awards ceremonies. Both participated in the 4th Annual DIRECTV Celebrity

KELLAN LUTZ, WHO PLAYS EMMETT CULLEN IN *TWILIGHT*, REMAINS GOOD
FRIENDS WITH TAYLOR.

Beach Bowl, competing against other celebrities and football legends.

Kellan and Taylor might be close, but Kellan has joked that Taylor keeps on trying to beat him up now that he has muscles. He thinks Taylor should give up because he'll never manage to beat him. We're not too sure: Kellan might be the biggest out of the two of them right now, but in a couple of years Taylor could easily catch up.

Kisses

Everyone remembers their first kiss and Taylor is no exception. He knows when, where and with whom, but that doesn't mean he's going to spill the beans to the whole world. The lucky girl must be kicking herself right now. Imagine letting Taylor out of your grasp.

In a very rare interview with *Seventeen* magazine, Taylor was asked how old he was when he had his first kiss. He said: 'It was some time in junior high. I don't remember what year, but it was definitely in junior high. I think it was just with a random girl from school. I mean, it's not like I walked up to her and was like, "You're just a random girl and I'm going to kiss you," but just a girl from school, and we had a little thing in junior high.'

It's clear that Taylor didn't want to divulge everything

about the kiss or the girl involved. He is just too respectful for that.

Many fans have dreamt about what it must be like to kiss Taylor, but if it was to happen and Taylor did kiss a fan, they would no doubt be very nervous. Actress Taylor Dooley had to kiss Taylor in *The Adventures of Sharkboy and Lavagirl 3-D* and she was really, really nervous. She only had to kiss him on the cheek, but because it was going to be her first kiss ever, she was on edge. The crew decided to pull a prank on her.

During the promotional tour of *The Adventures of Sharkboy and Lavagirl 3-D*, she told Michael J. Lee from RadioFree: 'I was really nervous and I was always telling the hair and make-up guy how nervous I was. It was only a peck on the cheek, but I was really nervous about it. So when I was in the schoolroom, he went and told Robert [Rodriguez, the director] that it was my first kiss and told him, "Do something really special." And Robert's like, [crafty] "Oh, don't worry, I will." So they call me onto set. And right before the kiss, he goes, "Sharkboy, off set! We're going to do the kiss. Bring in the stand-in."

'So they bring in this wooden post that is wrapped with green tape and he goes, "Kiss it like you're kissing Sharkboy." So I don't know what's going on and I'm kissing this piece of wood. I do it maybe two times, and he goes, "Okay, a little more, a little longer." And then I go to do it a fourth time and he starts cracking up, and then the whole set starts cracking up. And I'm sitting there, going, "Why is everyone laughing? Did I do something funny?" And he walks over to me and he gives me a hug, and he's like, "That was all a joke. I was gonna try to do it like fifty times, but I couldn't." So then I ended up having to kiss Sharkboy anyway [laughs].'

Poor Taylor, that was so mean of the crew to do that to her. At least Taylor had no idea what was going on: if he did, then he might have stopped the whole thing – he wouldn't have wanted his friend to be made a fool of.

It's not known how many girls Taylor has kissed, but he will have to kiss a lot more as his acting career continues to blossom. While filming the movie *Valentine's Day*, Taylor had to lose all his inhibitions and sweep Taylor Swift off her feet in a passionate embrace. They looked so good together that they were named Hottest On Screen Couple by Fandango – before *Valentine's Day* was even released in cinemas. Wow!

Kristen Stewart

Kristen Stewart is the actress who plays Bella in the *Twilight Saga* movies. She is someone Taylor was really happy to get the chance to work with and to become great friends with too.

Taylor told *MediaBlvd* magazine: 'Kristen's awesome!

KRISTEN AND TAYLOR
ARE GREAT FRIENDS
OFF SCREEN TOO.

She's an amazing actress and she's an awesome girl. She's a lot of fun. Everybody had good chemistry on this set.'

In many ways, Taylor and Kristen are as close friends as the characters they play. Although they might not be romantically linked like Jacob and Bella, they have the kind of friendship that will last forever. Taylor thinks Jacob's love for Bella is so intense that he will always be there for her, even if she picks Edward over him. Likewise, Taylor will always be there for Kristen, whoever she is dating.

Taylor might be closest to Kristen but he is also friends with Robert Pattinson. As he explained to *Interview* magazine: 'The whole cast is really close. It would be difficult for our characters, if we weren't. It's a love triangle, and we need to understand each other. So the fact that we're close and can talk things through in rehearsals, and if we're out at dinner, we'll just randomly start talking about the scene we're shooting the next day – if we weren't able to do those things, I don't know where we'd be.'

Taylor made sure that he was there for Kristen at the première of her movie, *The Runaways*, in March 2010. Sadly for Kristen, Robert Pattinson was in London promoting his own film, *Remember Me*, so he couldn't make it. Taylor, Kristen and Dakota Fanning all hung out together at *The Runaways* after-party and had a great time. In his leather jacket, black T-shirt and jeans,

Taylor looked really hot. The *Twilight* fans in the crowd all went crazy!

During a backstage interview, Kristen told the camera: 'I love Taylor. I'm so glad I look at someone every day and I believe every word that they say – it makes it impossible to fake anything.'

She has also talked to other interviewers about how special Taylor is and how great he was when he was surrounded by all the controversy before *New Moon* was filmed. She told About.com: 'I think that the controversy has probably been made bigger than it was. We needed to be sure that whoever played Jacob was going to be Jacob in *New Moon* – he's such a different person – he becomes a man. There's an entire [thing]. It's not just a physical transformation. He really becomes an adult. I mean, I always knew that Taylor could do that, but we just needed to make sure because it was so important. So once he actually proved himself, which wasn't hard to do, even seeing him walk around on set was like a different experience. He's literally become a different person: he's just grown up. He's so confident and the nicest guy that I've ever met. I know that I'm using this grammatically incorrect, but he's the funniest guy I've ever hung out with. So he's great. I'm so proud of him.'

It sounds like Kristen has a real soft spot for Taylor and sees him as a kind of younger brother.

Kristin Davis

Kristin Davis is the actress best known for playing Charlotte York in the *Sex and the City* TV shows and movies. She was fortunate enough to act alongside Taylor in *The Adventures of Sharkboy and Lavagirl 3-D* and is so pleased at the way things have turned out for him.

Kristin told MTV: 'He was the Sharkboy and I played the mother of the other kid who imagined Sharkboy and Lavagirl in Robert Rodriguez's movie, and I met him down in Texas. He was a kid and he didn't have those muscles, and I don't know what happened. I see these pictures [now and] I can't believe it. I feel protective, like what is he doing without his shirt on? And then I hear he's dating people and I'm like, "Ah!" [He was] nothing of those negative things that you think of with child actors. So for anyone to be succeeding, I'm happy for him.'

It's nice that Kristen has such fond memories of Taylor and wishes him well. He seems to have left a good impression on everyone who has ever worked with him. No one ever seems to have a bad word to say about him.

Taylor worked with Kristin on *The Adventures of Sharkboy and Lavagirl 3-D*.

L is for...

Love

It must be quite hard for Taylor to play someone who is so deeply in love in the *Twilight* movies and in *Valentine's Day* because he has never experienced what it's like to be in a long-term relationship. As far as we know, he has never been in love.

One day Taylor will hopefully be happily married like his parents are right now. It's great that he has parents who are deeply in love. He might not have found the love of his life just yet, but he will in the future.

Love, Inc.

In 2006, Taylor appeared in one episode of the sitcom *Love, Inc.* He played a character called Oliver in 'Arrested Development', but sadly the series was cancelled after only 22 episodes when the TV network merged with another.

Taylor doesn't generally mention this TV show when he talks about his previous roles, probably because he was only in the one episode.

M is for...

Max Steel

Ever since Taylor got his big muscles to play Jacob in *New Moon* he has been inundated with offers to be the next big action hero. In December 2009, it was announced that he would be playing the lead in *Max Steel*, a movie all about a 19-year-old extreme sports guy, who gets superhuman powers after an accident and is recruited by a secret agency.

This would have been the perfect role for the sports-mad Taylor, but sadly it wasn't to be. Because *Max Steel* is based on an action figure by Mattel, it is rumoured Taylor had to drop out because he wants to be in a *Stretch Armstrong* movie based on a rival company's toy.

Taylor's decision to pull out of *Max Steel* has split his fans down the middle. One fan wrote on the taylorlautnersource.com wall: 'I would've stayed with *Max Steel*. I'm not sure I'm so into seeing Taylor's arms stretched out. I imagine it may come off really lame.' Another wrote: 'Taylor might be doing too much at once. Maybe it's a good thing for him to drop out of this role. Anyway, I would rather see him in more personal roles like a leading man in a major movie. He is a very talented performer and I am looking forward to seeing a lot more of him in the right roles.'

What do you think? Would you rather see Taylor in *Max Steel* or *Stretch Armstrong*?

Mike Chat

One of Taylor's heroes when he first started karate was Mike Chat. In 1999, when Taylor was seven, he got to meet Mike for the first time. His karate teacher Sensei Tom Fabiano had entered him for his first tournament in Louisville, Kentucky. Taylor managed to impress everyone, including Mike, with his routines. Chat recognised that Taylor was something special and invited him to his Camp Chat International Summer School, an offer that Taylor couldn't refuse.

TAYLOR SHOWS OFF SOME OF HIS MOVES.

It was at the camp that Taylor fell in love with the Mike Chat style of martial arts. There, he was taught more martial arts skills, gymnastics, acrobatics and stunt training. He left with a burning desire to learn more and the ability to do aerial cartwheels without needing to use his hands.

Taylor did so well at the camp that Mike decided that he should become his instructor. Sensei Tom Fabiano stepped down – he knew that Taylor would be able to develop even more under Mike.

Mike Chat's full name is Michael Chaturantabut and he is a Thai-American actor and martial arts expert. He is best known for playing Chad Lee, the Blue Power Ranger in *Power Rangers: Lightspeed Rescue*. Mike is so good at martial arts that he was inducted into the World Martial Arts Wall of Fame in 1992 and during his career he has won over 50 championships.

Mike might have been the best instructor that Taylor could have dreamt of, but he didn't live anywhere near him. He couldn't just pop down to his karate school, as he had been able to do with Tom Fabiano. Instead, he had to try and schedule time in with Mike whenever he could. This was quite tricky because Mike was often away travelling to different competitions and set locations. Also, Taylor couldn't afford to miss school because his parents wanted him to do well academically.

At the time, Taylor told karateangels.com: 'I try to get with my instructor, Mike Chat, as much as possible. He gives me homework assignments to work on at home. Then I go out with my Mom and Dad's help in trying to achieve my homework from Mike.'

Since Taylor's acting career has taken off, he's had to stop doing extreme martial arts training with Mike, but he still practises his moves to keep his body supple. He had to stop training so hard because he needed to put on weight to play Jacob Black in *New Moon* and if he'd continued with his martial arts training, this would have been impossible.

Taylor owes Mike Chat so much that he'll be forever be a great teacher and a great friend. He's been snapped by paparazzi photographers going for lunch with Mike and catching up with him in Los Angeles when he's on breaks from filming the *Twilight Saga* movies.

Modelling

Unlike his *Twilight* co-stars Robert Pattinson, Kellan Lutz and Cam Gigandet, Taylor has never done any modelling. He was so busy with his martial arts and acting as a kid that he never really had the time to do some modelling shoots as well – he had to do school work instead!

Since he got his new buff body for *New Moon*, people have been seeing Taylor in a whole new light and it's thought that he might soon be modelling for some of the

Taylor's good looks make him a shoo-in for any international fashion designer.

world's biggest brands. Lots of fans would love to see him modelling designer underwear!

On 9 December 2009, it was reported that Taylor was in negotiations for a contract with Giorgio Armani. It was rumoured that he would be the new face and body of a new aftershave and a clothing line called A/X Armani Exchange. As of yet, nothing has been confirmed, but if Taylor did do a deal with the designer, then he would be in line for quite a large paycheck. He would, after all, be following in the footsteps of former England football captain David Beckham!

Movies

You can't be a big movie star and not enjoy watching movies. Every actor and actress loves sitting on their sofa with some popcorn and watching a movie with their loved ones, away from the prying eyes of photographers and the media. Taylor is no different and he likes to watch movies whenever he can.

He really enjoys watching Golden Globe winner Tom Cruise in *The Last Samurai*. It's one of his favourite movies of all time and he has watched it so often. Taylor explained to ultimatedisney.com: 'I love that movie – I guess I kind of like it because I can relate to it. I started out with the traditional Japanese martial arts and then I went into the extreme new modern version. In that movie, they started out with the samurai and the traditional fighting in war, and then they go to the more modern one. So I guess I could relate to it well and it just got me really in the moment. And I thought that Tom Cruise did a great job portraying that role.'

The other films that Taylor likes to watch are ones starring Denzel Washington, Matt Damon and Brad Pitt. He used to have a bit of a crush on Jessica Alba and joked to Tyra Banks during an interview that he was dating her, but he now has a bit of a thing for *Transformers* star Megan Fox.

Taylor will watch pretty much any type of movie: comedy, romance, horror… but his favourites tend to be action types such as *Iron Man* and the *Bourne* series. He thought Christian Bale and Heath Ledger were superb in *The Dark Knight*.

Taylor never wants to be typecast and hopes that he will be able to play roles in lots of different movie genres. Action dramas will always be his favourite but he's eager to follow in the footsteps of Ryan Reynolds and Gerard Butler and do a romantic comedy or two. His fans would love to watch him in rom-coms the most because they love seeing Taylor's sensitive, loving side and they could close their eyes and pretend that he's serenading them instead of the female character on screen.

The movie that Taylor is a bit embarrassed to admit he

TOM CRUISE IS THE STAR OF TAYLOR'S FAVOURITE FILM, *THE LAST SAMURAI*.

loves is *The Notebook*. It's a very romantic movie and stars Rachel McAdams and Ryan Gosling. The movie's tagline is: 'Behind every great love is a great story'. It certainly isn't a manly film, but it's such a beautiful story that we can't blame Taylor for secretly loving it.

Music Videos

Taylor hasn't only been in movies and TV shows. He's also appeared in a couple of music videos. He starred in the music video of Cassi Thomson's first single 'Caught Up In You'. Taylor played the boy that Cassi can't stop thinking about and they share a kiss right at the end. Lucky Cassi!

Taylor has also made his own music video for the track 'Apologize' by *OneRepublic*, which is well worth checking out on YouTube. He might be miming in it, but it's really good. It's thought that it was made for a school assignment so he should have got full marks! It's awesome and Taylor looks so sexy in it. The girl in the video is his good friend Sara Hicks.

My Own Worst Enemy

My Own Worst Enemy was a short-lived television series starring Christian Slater and Taylor that came out in

Taylor appears in Cassi Thomson's music video, 'Caught Up In You'.

October 2008. Taylor started shooting it as soon as filming for *Twilight* wrapped. Naturally, he and the rest of the cast had hoped that it would be a massive hit and several series might be made. Ultimately, only nine episodes were made so no one would ever find out what happened to Christian Slater's character Edward Albright.

Taylor must have been gutted when the show was cancelled as he had put a lot of hard work into preparing and filming the seven episodes that he appeared in. He really liked playing Jack Spivey, the varsity soccer player son of Christian Slater's character. Instead of taking a long, well deserved rest after *Twilight* finished like many of the other actors, he had started filming *My Own Worst Enemy* two days a week.

If you missed seeing *My Own Worst Enemy* when it was on TV, you can buy the whole series on DVD. It's well worth checking out because Taylor gets to use some of his martial arts skills – and looks super-hot as well!

My Wife and Kids

Taylor might have only been in just one episode of *My Wife and Kids* in 2004, but he really enjoyed himself. He found it nice to be working on a comedy show even though he was playing a bully called Tyrone.

The episode Taylor was in was called 'Class Reunion'.

In it, he bullies the youngest son of the family, Kady Kyle, and gets a big surprise. Basically, what happens is that Kady goes to the park where he's bullied by Taylor's character and two other bullies. As they push him around, he warns that if they don't stop then he'll eat a pill that turns him into a monster. But they ignore him and so he starts to chew the pill, pretends to shake and goes into a nearby toilet. As Tyrone (Taylor) and the other bullies go to follow him, a huge man wearing identical clothes to what Kady was wearing (but torn), comes out, saying, 'I warned you!' The bullies start to scream and run off.

Shortly after filming his scenes, Taylor told kidsworld.com: 'I got to be a bully and push this little kid around. That was fun because I'm normally not a bully because my parents wouldn't allow me to do that. I'm just not that person, but it was fun to experience something new.'

N is for...

Naked

Not only does Taylor Lautner have the hottest body out of all the actors in the *Twilight Saga* movies, but he also has the hottest body of pretty much any actor in Hollywood right now. Zac Efron might have worked out to get his chest looking toned for *17 Again*, but he has nothing on Taylor.

Taylor didn't mind having to strip off to play Jacob Black and would get half-naked again in other movies, if the roles required it. He'll no doubt be showing off more of his body if he does romantic comedies in the future and might even have to do a few scenes completely naked!

Taylor's favourite Jacob line from any of the *Twilight Saga* books is from *New Moon*. It's when Jacob asks, 'Does my half being naked bother you?' He told MTV: 'That quote just cracks me up. Because you know, that's when he's shirtless, not wearing a top.' He really enjoyed saying that line when they filmed *New Moon*.

It was actually quite embarrassing for Taylor to take off his shirt in front of the *New Moon* cast and crew. Also, knowing that millions of *Twilight* fans around the world would see him half-naked when the movie hit cinemas freaked him out a bit too. He must have known that his body would become a big talking point. He says it was also a bit awkward for his mum, dad and sister, but he's glad they haven't teased him about it because he'd go bright red.

For Taylor, the most embarrassing *Twilight* scene to watch back is the one after Bella's motorcycle accident, when Jacob takes off his top and uses it to mop up the blood on Bella's forehead. He explained to iesb.com: 'I start laughing so hard, every time I see that scene. "You're bleeding? Okay, let me fix it." It's so embarrassing! Here's the thing: there's a reason that he's not wearing clothes, all the time. One: when he transforms, all his clothes get shredded – he can't help it. And when he goes into the woods to get something to put on, so that he's not naked, it's just a ripped pair of jean shorts. He's also hot – he's 108 degrees. So, that's another reason. The thing is, I love this character and story, and putting on the weight and not wearing much clothing was required by the role. A year from now, if I love a story and I love a character that requires me to lose forty pounds, I'm ready to do it!'

New Moon

For Taylor, being able to play Jacob Black in *New Moon* was a dream come true. He had worked so hard to be physically able to play the role that it would have broken his heart if he had lost out. Also, he loved being back with the cast and working with new director Chris Weitz.

In *New Moon* Taylor got to do more stunts than he had done before in any other movie. He really appreciated how much Chris Weitz trusted him and let him do stunts. Other directors might have called in the stuntmen, but because Taylor was so fit and able to do flips and twists because of his martial arts training, Chris let him try.

Taylor enjoyed filming *New Moon* so much that he can't decide which scene he liked best. He told Talia Soghomonian from the *Metro News*: 'It's so hard to choose – I really enjoy the stunts so I had a lot of fun doing the dirt bike sequences. I got to hop on the bike and go really fast and come to a skidding stop. It's really cool. And I also like a lot of the more serious scenes: the pivotal scenes in the movie, like Jacob and Bella's break-up scene, which is the first time Bella sees Jacob after he has transformed into a wolf and it's really emotional. I felt bad for Jacob just reading the books, but now that I'm actually living this character, I feel so bad for the guy! It's really sad.'

People might think that actors have an easy life, shoot a few scenes and get paid a lot of money to travel the world, but it's actually quite hard going. Because Taylor was in so many of the scenes in *New Moon*, he had to get up at 4.30 or 5am each day, rush to the set and then stay there until 5 or 6pm. He'd then grab something to eat in one of the Vancouver restaurants with the rest of the cast, go back to his hotel room, study the script for the next day and try and get some sleep.

When Taylor was filming *Twilight* there were always a few fans of the books hanging around the sets to watch, but when *New Moon* was being made there were a whole lot more. The fans would stay for hours and hours in freezing conditions, but they wouldn't mind – they just wanted to catch a glimpse of Taylor and the rest of the cast arriving and leaving the set. Sometimes they would wait until 7am if there was an overnight shoot going on.

Taylor divulged to *Interview* magazine: 'It's the weirdest thing. Nobody really saw it coming. I mean, we knew we were making a movie of a very popular book, but we didn't know how well it was going to do. When it opened, it exploded, and that was not something any of us saw coming. Filming *New Moon* is a lot different than the

TWILIGHT FANS CAMPED OVERNIGHT DURING THE FILMING OF *TWILIGHT: NEW MOON* JUST TO CATCH A GLIMPSE OF THEIR FAVOURITE STARS.

first one because this time we know what we are getting into. It puts a little more pressure on us than it did before. But for the most part, it's been a blast.'

Northern Lights

In January 2010 it was rumoured that Taylor would be playing Tom Cruise's son in a big blockbuster called *Northern Lights*. It was suggested that he would receive a whopping $7.5 million, but this was never officially confirmed.

A few days later a movie rep revealed the film's official

logline – a logline is a brief description of what happens in a film, similar to the blurb on the back of a book. They said: 'Set against the backdrop of extreme flying, *Northern Lights* follows four young pilots as they compete against the world's best. A story of teamwork, sacrifice, loss and victory, these young aviators push themselves to physical and emotional limits in the unforgiving world of performance aerobatics.'

Sadly for Taylor fans, on 22 February it was reported that he had dropped out of *Northern Lights*. No official statement was released to explain why, but some websites suggest that Taylor is too busy with the other upcoming movie projects.

O is for...

Oregon

Taylor had to move from Los Angeles to Oregon in 2008 for several months while *Twilight* was being filmed. It must have been a bit of a culture shock moving from a place where it's sunny 320 days per year on average to Portland, Oregon, where it's mostly mild and moist. Also, it must have been hard leaving home and moving into a hotel room instead. At least the young *Twilight* cast had each other for company and could stop anyone from feeling too homesick by going out all the time.

The unpredictable Oregon weather was a real challenge for *Twilight* director Catherine Hardwicke and the rest of the cast and crew. While promoting *Twilight*, Taylor told GoneWithTheTwins.com: 'I filmed a scene on the beach with my wannabe girlfriend and wardrobe had originally just picked out jeans and a T-shirt for us, and we got there and there was sleet, hail... It was pouring rain, freezing-cold 40 mile-per-hour winds, the tide was up to our knees – it was insane. We filmed the whole thing that way and we ended up wearing several pairs of socks, a couple pairs of jeans, sweatshirts, ponchos, beanies, mittens, everything. The weather was pretty challenging.'

Even though the beach scene in the movie ended up being a lot different to the one in Stephenie Meyer's book *Twilight*, the fans still love it. Taylor does too: 'This is going to sound weird, but the beach scene was my favourite scene. It was painful, I was hating it, but at the same time, looking back at it, it was a lot of fun finishing every take and huddling over a little heater, and having our hot chocolate to warm us up. It was my least favourite and my favourite.'

Filming days in Oregon were often very long: because of the changing weather, scenes had to be constantly re-shot. This wasn't a pleasurable experience for Taylor: 'We did every scene, every angle, everything with the hideous weather up until about 2:00. Then the sun randomly appears and it stops raining and they say, "Let's do everything again." So we do everything again, and sure enough, they use the nice weather in the film.'

Journalists who travelled to Oregon to interview Taylor, Rob and Kristen also had problems because of the weather. Taylor recalls: 'I did an interview under a tent and literally, while they were filming, this girl was in high heels and the wind blows and the tent comes up and flies over our heads and she falls down!'

Even though the weather was unpredictable, the cast enjoyed filming in Oregon because there were plenty of restaurants and places to hang out. It was also the place where they got to know each other and bonded. It must have been hard for them to leave it behind when Vancouver was named the location for *New Moon* filming.

Oscars

At the 2009 Oscars it was Robert Pattinson who was the man of the moment, but it was Taylor's turn to shine as he presented alongside Kristen Stewart at the 2010 Oscars.

On the red carpet Taylor admitted: 'It's amazing, it's totally surreal to actually be here after watching it on TV growing up. It's an honour. I had to get a suit, definitely had to do that – you know not too much [to prepare]. I'm just thrilled to be here. It's going to be a great night.'

After the ceremony finished, Taylor attended the *Vanity Fair* Oscar Party, which is one of the parties most sought-after by the big stars. It was held at the Sunset Tower Hotel

aylor is mobbed by
s fans at the première
Twilight: Eclipse.

Our favourite actor attends a *Twilight* fan party.

Above: Taylor had amazing on screen chemistry with *Twilight* co-star Kristen Stewart.

Right: Taylor is said to be one of the nicest guys in the business.

Left: Taylor arrives at the *Twilight: Eclipse* première in New York City.

Right: Our favourite actor answers questions at yet another movie première.

aylor won a 'Teen Choice Award' in the Choice Movie Fresh Face Male tegory in 2009, and has been a regular attendee at the annual event.

Above: Taylor and his *Twilight* co-stars appear on 'Jimmy Kimmel Live' to promote *Twilight: New Moon*.

Below: Fans on the red carpet try to attract our favourite actor's attention at the L.A. première of *Twilight: Eclipse*.

Above: Taylor meets fans outside the Kimmel theatre in L.A.

Left: Taylor's co-star and on-screen *Twilight* rival, Robert Pattinson.

Taylor and Kristen have become
really close friends ever since the
Twilight saga began

TAYLOR LOOKED
THE PART WHEN HE
ATTENDED THE 2010
OSCAR CEREMONY.

and there he mingled with Tom Hanks, Amy Adams, Hilary Swank, Sean Penn and a whole host of other famous names. Thankfully, Kristen Stewart was also at the party so Taylor could always talk to her if he got star-struck!

However, the Oscars weren't the first awards show where Taylor has presented: he also did some presenting at the Golden Globes when he introduced the movie *500 Days of Summer*. Taylor did so well that he might be asked to present an actual award next year – that's if he isn't up for one himself. He is so talented that he could end up winning several Oscars and Golden Globes in the next decade or two.

P is for...

Pilot

When he was younger, Taylor did a pilot for a TV show called *Which Way Is Up?*, but it was never made into a TV series. He had the main part and so he must have been a bit gutted when it didn't get the go-ahead – he didn't let it get him down, though, and instead kept going for bigger and better auditions.

Premières

Taylor might have been just thirteen years old at *The Adventures of Sharkboy and Lavagirl 3-D* première, but he wasn't overwhelmed or nervous when he stood on the red carpet. He had attended five premières before, including the Matthew McConaughey movie *Sahara* and John Travolta's film *Ladder 49*. With the rest of the cast and crew, he had already watched the finished movie of *The Adventures of Sharkboy and Lavagirl* beforehand and so he must have known that it was a good film and that the young kids would love it.

Taylor told Mark Sells from the *Oregon Herald*: 'It was fun watching how much fun we had on the set and how it turned out as a movie – it made me think of all the memories and moments from all the different scenes we shot. Walking the red carpet, you wouldn't believe how many photographers are there! "Taylor, turn over here. Turn to the right, hold it here, to the left, now over here…" It's really crazy on the red carpet, but knowing that it was your première made it even more fun.'

Whenever Taylor attends premieres he likes to have a friendly face with him and will often take along one of his relatives. At first he had to do this because he was a child and needed an adult with him, but even now he still likes to share his red-carpet experiences with the people who mean the most to him.

Shortly before the *Twilight* première, Taylor shared this with *Teen Mag*: 'I'm having one of my grandparents come out for the movie and they're actually going to the première. All of my family lives in Michigan and every family member has read the books – I mean all four of my grandparents, aunts, and uncles, everybody! It's just crazy cool that they love it so much!'

Taylor might have been as cool as a cucumber at the première of *The Adventures of Sharkboy and Lavagirl 3-D*, but this proved impossible at the *Twilight* première. There were too many screaming girls, over 3,000 of them wanting to get his autograph. The *New Moon* première was even bigger: an estimated 10,000 fans turned up. Taylor could have taken any girl he wanted as his date, but he took his little sister Makena instead. He's so kind and generous – not many brothers would do that for their sisters.

Each *Twilight Saga* movie brings more and more fans to the premières, so who knows how many will turn up to the final movie, *Breaking Dawn...*

Preparation

Every good actor knows that preparation is key and it's not good enough just to relax once you've secured a role. Keen to do a convincing performance of a member of the Quileute tribe, Taylor really wanted to play the best Jacob Black he could and he told Adrienne Gaffney from *Vanity Fair*: 'Before I went up to Portland, I did some research on the Quileute tribe. I set up a meeting with some real

Quileute tribal members in Portland and I got to meet and talk with them. To my surprise, I learned that they are just like me. What they love is sports and girls.'

In addition to this, Taylor read everything he could about the Quileute tribe, their myths and legends. He also read Stephenie Meyer's books over and over because he knew that he must be the Jacob Black that the fans had fallen in love with in the first place, that he had to act within the restrictions already in place. The fans would have hated his performance, had he totally reinvented who Jacob was and what he was about.

Presenting

Taylor might only be young, but he has already shown that he has great presenting skills. Aside from the Oscars and the Golden Globes, he has had plenty of other presenting opportunities, too.

At the 2009 MTV Video Music Awards in New York, Taylor presented the Best Female Video Award with Shakira. It ended up being quite a memorable moment – but not for the right reasons.

Taylor got his lines right, announced that Taylor Swift had won, gave his close friend a congratulatory hug and then stepped to the side of the stage to allow Taylor to make her acceptance speech. As she attempted to do so,

KANYE WEST AT THE MTV MUSIC VIDEO AWARDS IN 2009

though, an angry Kanye West jumped onto the stage and announced that Beyoncé's video was 'one of the greatest of all time.' Shell-shocked, poor Taylor was unable to continue.

A few months later when our favourite actor was asked to host the late-night sketch show *Saturday Night Live*, he jumped at the chance – plus the opportunity to level the score. He did a fantastic sketch with two dummies, one dressed as Taylor Swift and the other as Kanye West. Taylor asked the Taylor Swift doll what was wrong and then told the audience that he was going to do what he should have done at the MTV VMAs: he took off his jacket, did a back flip, then showed off his martial arts skills by kicking and jabbing in the direction of the Kanye dummy. When he narrowly missed Kanye's head with one of his kicks, he decided to use his hand to knock the head off. He then picked it up and stuck it back on. The audience squealed with delight as Taylor then went over to the Taylor Swift dummy and leant in as if he was going to kiss her.

Taylor did so well in presenting the *Saturday Night Live* show that he'll no doubt be asked to host it again and maybe even host bigger shows and events in the future. He shows great potential as he never forgets his lines or seems fazed by big audiences.

Q is for...

Quileute Language

As well as meeting members of the Quileute tribe while preparing to play Jacob Black, Taylor also learnt how to speak like them. There are only four people in the whole world who can speak the Quileute language so it was a great honour and privilege for Taylor to be entrusted to speak their language in *New Moon*.

He told Fred Topel from *CanMag*: 'I did speak a little bit of Quileute, when I was leaning in to kiss her [Bella] in the kitchen, and no, I'm not gonna tell you what I said. I'll leave that to you to figure out, but it was really cool.'

If you want to know what Jacob says to Bella in

Quileute, we've found it out for you: he says, 'Stay with me forever.'

As well as speaking the Quileute language, Taylor also wanted to show the Quileute spirit in his performance. Through meeting them, he realised that they go out of their way to help one another. If a job needs doing around the house, then they will do it without being asked. Friendships are important to them and they will do anything for someone they care about. Taylor really wanted to convey this in the way he portrayed Jacob.

But Taylor wasn't the only one who wanted to portray the Quileute tribe correctly in the *Twilight Saga* movies. *New Moon* director Chris Weitz told *Entertainment Weekly*: 'When prepping to visualize Jacob's and Emily's houses, production designer David Brisbin and his team visited La Push and met the Quileute executive council. While they were there, a young Quileute girl gave David the first drum she made (this is a Quileute custom). To show appreciation, we decided to put the drum in a prominent shot – it's at the entrance of Emily's house, and you see it when Bella first enters. Also, the high-pitched 'call' that Embry and Jared give when they jump out of Bella's car is a thing the Quileute kids do.'

The authentic way that the Quileute tribe is portrayed in *New Moon* and the other *Twilight Saga* movies is a real credit to Taylor, Chris, David and the rest of the *Twilight* team.

R is for...

Rain

Chris Weitz had to bring in fake rain to shoot the scene in *New Moon* when Bella confronts Jacob. Catherine Hardwicke might have had too much rain during the shooting of *Twilight*, but Chris had the opposite problem when he was shooting in Vancouver. The fake rain from the machine was sometimes too heavy and Kristen Stewart struggled to get her words out. Indeed, she had to stop one take because she felt as if she was drowning. Chris had to keep experimenting with the rain levels to make sure the right look was created on camera that also wouldn't prevent the actors from being able to deliver their lines.

DIRECTOR CHRIS WEITZ WITH TAYLOR, KRISTEN AND ROB.

Kristen might have been able to wear clothes during the fake rain scene, but Taylor wasn't so lucky. As he explained to *ET*: 'When I'm in this 38-degree weather and I'm naked almost and it's pouring rain on me, I can't seem like I'm cold, I can't be shivering, because Jacob's supposed to be just perfectly fine in it.'

The whole crew was impressed with the way Taylor managed to keep going and was able to shoot the scene over and over again without complaining. Many actors in his shoes would have demanded comfort breaks to get warm again, but he didn't.

Despite Taylor and Kristen's discomfort, Chris felt it was really important to have the rain for that particular scene. The director explained: 'It's just one of those great romantic, high-tension scenes where the atmosphere builds to support the emotions of the moment, so what might otherwise have been just an argument between friends becomes this very charged situation.'

Robert Pattinson

Taylor's biggest rival will always be British actor Robert Pattinson. They divide the *Twilight* fan base because half of the fans love Jacob, while the other half loves Edward. Only a very few sit on the fence and love both actors.

Taylor might be well built, but he isn't sure who would win if he fought Robert. He may look tougher than Robert, but he isn't 100 per cent sure of the result. He told Movies.About.com: 'Oh man, I don't know between me and Rob – he actually does a lot of boxing in his time off; it might be a good match-up. We were actually discussing this onset: it's funny, like, who would win in a fight between Jacob and Edward? Because there's a scene outside Bella's house where Edward grabs my shoulder and Jacob doesn't take that, so he takes his arm

TWILIGHT CO-STAR
AND ON-SCREEN
RIVAL, ROBERT
PATTINSON.

and rips it off, and that moment Jacob would transform into a wolf.

And we're having this discussion, it got really deep, we were like, "If I were to poof into a wolf right now, what would happen? Who would win?" Our discussion points were, we're usually with our pack so if I'm without my pack, am I going to be weaker? Honestly, I don't know. That discussion is still up in the air. We should probably get Stephenie Meyer on the line and ask her.'

But Robert disagrees: he thinks Taylor would win because he's seen the martial arts videos of him when he was nine and he thinks that he would need some kind of weapon to be able to compete with Taylor in a fight.

Taylor and Robert might be big rivals on-screen, but they get on really well in real life. They enjoy hanging out on and off set with Kristen Stewart, too. Taylor thinks that their good chemistry off set helps them to portray their characters' close friendships in the *Twilight* movies.

When Taylor arrived on the *New Moon* set, looking all buff, the rest of the cast were gob-smacked. Robert Pattinson admits that he felt inferior and says of that time: 'I hadn't worked out at all until I saw Taylor at the beginning of the year. I felt incredibly inadequate and emasculated. I had a pre-pubescent teen body – I had A-cups!'

Many people might think that Robert has the best part in *Twilight*, but the British actor would love to play Jacob instead. He told Taylor: 'I've always wanted your part – even when we're doing scenes together!'

Taylor wouldn't want to play Edward, though. If he wasn't playing Jacob, then he would like to play Bella instead. He replied: 'Is Bella an option? I would love to get inside Bella's mind. A lot of weird things are going on in there – I would love to experience that!'

Robert Rodriguez

One of the first directors that Taylor got to work with was Robert Rodriguez and he remains one of his favourite directors. Rodriguez directed Taylor in *The Adventures of Sharkboy and Lavagirl 3-D*. He has also directed Jessica Alba in *Sin City* and Bruce Willis in *Planet Terror*.

Taylor explained to the *Oregon Herald*: 'What's so amazing about Robert is that he directs his films, he writes them, he edits them, and he's even the cameraman. Best of all, he's a terrific pizza maker. He makes the best pizza! In his house, he has this big stone oven. It's about 15 feet tall and he makes the most incredible pizza and ravioli!'

Robert was a really relaxed director, who wanted his young actors and actresses to have lots of fun while they were filming. He would play video games with them and let them go on his boat after filming finished; he didn't shout at them when they got things wrong but instead encouraged them. At first, this shocked Taylor as he was used to his football and karate instructors shouting at him.

Taylor added: 'He's such a great director. While shooting a lot of scenes with the green screen (the background would be added later using computer animation) he would tell us exactly what was going on, painting the picture in our heads of what it's supposed to look like and what we're supposed to be doing.'

Rugrats Go Wild

In 2003, Taylor was thrilled when his voice was used in an advertisement for the film *Rugrats Go Wild*. Though he might not have had many lines, he was delighted just to have a paid job. He had been to so many auditions and got nowhere, so it must have been nice to be wanted for a change.

Taylor admits: 'It was my first job – I was so ecstatic. I thought, "This is what I've been waiting for!"'

Rumours

Every famous actor has to get used to people making up rumours about them to sell magazines and newspapers.

DIRECTOR ROBERT RODRIGUEZ WORKED WITH TAYLOR ON *THE ADVENTURES OF SHARKBOY AND LAVAGIRL 3-D.*

Sometimes the actors will fight back and sue those magazines that print false stories, but Taylor hasn't had to take such drastic action just yet. Instead, he has decided to ignore the rumours by not bothering to read any of the gossip websites or magazines. Taylor told iesb.com: 'Honestly, I try to stay away from what has been written about me because if you let that stuff get to you and it's not true, it can drive you crazy. One thing that I have heard recently, which is not true and I definitely didn't say it, was when I was quoted as saying I will never take my shirt off for a movie again. If I have to, and the character requires it, I will. Who knows? In 10 years, I might do that – it's just what the character requires. So, that was interesting to see.'

Taylor has actually been quite lucky because none of the rumours about him have been too serious. Poor Robert Pattinson has been falsely accused of having a drink problem and taking a drug overdose.

On April Fool's Day, two rumours were circulating about Taylor and across the globe, many of his fans believed what they were reading. The stories said that Taylor won't be in *Breaking Dawn* after all and that he planned to pose nude for *Playgirl Magazine*. Needless to say, there wasn't a shred of truth in either story.

S is for...

School

Taylor's first school was called Jamestown Elementary School and it was there that he first developed his passion for sport. He has always been a team player and he joined lots of clubs, which kept him really busy and out of trouble: he was in the wrestling club, the martial arts club, the football team and the baseball team. Eventually Taylor had to drop some of them because he couldn't do everything; that must have been hard because he loved being in all the different clubs and teams.

By the time Taylor was eight he was juggling his martial arts training with his school work and school clubs. He had to work so hard to make sure that he didn't fall behind the other students in his class when he attended movie auditions.

Taylor said at the time: 'I get mostly A's, with an occasional A-minus here and there. The key is an open communication with my teacher. My parents and me are in close communication with my teachers to make sure I'm not missing anything and understanding assignments. This doesn't mean it's not been difficult, because it has. I think once the school understands that my education is important to me then they are more understanding. The last week has been really tough – I've had to stay up till 10.30 or 11pm each night to make sure all my homework is done.'

Poor Taylor! He must have been so tired in the mornings, having to get up early for school, when he'd much rather be catching up on some sleep.

Having to go to school was actually the worst thing about being a child actor, according to Taylor. He told UltimateDisney.com: 'you gotta do school three hours a day and sometimes more because they want to bank hours. At the end of the movie, if you don't have enough time or if you want to relax more, you're going to be leaving in a couple of days, then you get to use some of your bank hours – that's pretty much how it works.'

Selena Gomez

The Disney actress and singer Selena Gomez is one of Taylor's closest friends. She might be younger than him, but she is just as experienced: Selena has been in several movies and TV series, including *Barney & Friends*, *Wizards of Waverly Place: The Movie*, *Hannah Montana* and *Another Cinderella Story*.

When Taylor was filming *New Moon* in Vancouver, he and Selena hung out a lot together in the city. But Selena didn't make the trip to Canada just to meet Taylor for the first time, she was filming *Ramona and Beezus* (an adaptation of Beverly Cleary's popular children's books) there too, and so it made sense that they went out to eat together and to watch a movie at the local cinema. Sometimes other members of the *New Moon* cast also came along, but the paparazzi photographers just focused on Selena and Taylor all the time. Magazines printed photos of them linking arms and hugging, which suggested they were dating, but they are just good friends who enjoy spending time together, nothing more.

Selena revealed all about their friendship to *Seventeen* magazine: 'Kristen [Stewart] was staying in my hotel. He would visit her, so we were constantly running into each other in the lobby – and we ended up meeting. We would go out to lunch and dinner, but I knew he had paparazzi

SELENA AND TAYLOR ARE JUST CLOSE FRIENDS.

following him and I had paparazzi following me. So we literally just wanted to hang out, go bowling and stuff, and it went a little too far, I think. People were getting a little crazy about us.

'But it was fun – I went to Vancouver thinking I was going to focus on my work, but instead I got to meet him, and it ended up being the best thing ever. He is so sweet, Taylor has made me so happy – I didn't know I could be that happy. You probably see it in the pictures! I'm smiling so big.'

It's great that Taylor and Selena hit it off straight away and have become really close friends. And it's very rare to find a friend that will be your friend forever, whatever happens, but it looks like Taylor has found someone who is just that. It is great that Selena is famous too, so she can give Taylor advice and help him when the pressure gets too much.

Maybe one day they could act together on a romantic comedy. Many Taylor and Selena fans would be thrilled because they look so great together and their chemistry is very real.

Shadow Fury

Taylor's first movie was called *Shadow Fury*. It was a sci-fi film made for TV and so it wasn't shown at cinemas. On 30 October 2001, it was released in Japan.

Taylor plays the part of Kismet, a small child. The story centres on a bounty hunter who has to stop a ruthless ninja clone from murdering innocent people. Nickelodeon and iCarly star Jennette McCurdy also appeared in the movie. She played a girl called Anna Markov. *Shadow Fury* is available to buy on DVD but being an 18, it might not be suitable for the majority of Taylor's fans.

Silas and Brittany

Taylor voiced Silas in the Disney cartoon, *Silas and Brittany*. It was a series about a cat and a dog. This could have been a really good break for Taylor, but the show didn't have a long run.

He told UltimateDisney.com: 'I definitely love film and live acting better than voiceover, but I do a lot of voiceover stuff and, you know what, I love both. I like live acting and I love voiceover because you're not on camera and usually, you're playing a person totally opposite of yourself and you just get to change your voice and be a weird character, and that's an awful lot of fun.'

Sadly there are no videos of *Silas and Brittany* available on the Internet or even an image, so apart from the few lucky fans who managed to watch it when it first aired, no one will know what it was like. Unless Disney decides to repeat the show, we'll probably never get the opportunity to watch it – that's a real shame because virtually all of the other shows that Taylor has done are available to watch online or on DVD.

Smoking

Unlike his *Twilight Saga* co-stars Robert Pattinson and Kristen Stewart, Taylor has never tried smoking a cigarette, let alone taken up such a bad habit. What's more, he has never smoked pot, snorted a line of cocaine or done any other form of illegal drugs, unlike so many other young Hollywood stars these days. Taylor is far too sensible to risk his health by doing something so stupid. He's a great role model for young kids as he is forever striving to be the best and looks after his body – you won't ever see him checking into rehab.

Stephenie Meyer

Taylor would have never been able to play Jacob Black, had Stephenie Meyer not had a dream about a vampire and a young girl in a meadow. Stephenie's dream, on 2 June 2003, was so vivid that when she woke up, she decided that she needed to write it all down and so *Twilight* was born. The

TWILIGHT CREATOR STEPHENIE MEYER WAS INSTRUMENTAL IN TAYLOR
GETTING THE ROLE OF JACOB BLACK.

character of Jacob was borne out of Stephenie's research into the Quileute tribe shortly after deciding that the town of Forks, Washington was where the story should be set. Each evening, when her three young boys were tucked up in bed, she would work on her book and three months later, it was finished.

The name Jacob is very special to Stephenie because it is the name of one of her brothers.

Before Taylor was cast as Jacob Black, Stephenie admitted that she would like the actor, model and singer Steven Strait to play Jacob – she had been discussing who the fans thought should play the main roles on her official website. She wrote: 'And finally, I found my favorite Jacob Black, though he's a *New Moon*-aged Jacob (which means he'd be way, way too old to ever play Jacob, if they ever made *New Moon* into a movie. Sigh. This is sort of what Jacob looks like in my head, though) – Steven Strait.'

Even though Stephenie first wanted Steven to play Jacob, she was delighted when she got to meet Taylor and she saw his great acting ability. She must have known straight away that he could pull off the role.

Taylor really enjoys meeting Stephenie whenever she visits the set or when they are attending the different premières. He told a journalist from the *Metro News* during their set visit: 'It's really cool because she comes up here every once in a while for her favourite scenes. At the beginning of filming, she gives a list of her favourite scenes that she wants to be up here for. You've got the best person in the world to ask for advice, so if you have a question, you can just walk on over and ask her.'

After Stephenie saw *New Moon* being filmed, she told one fan: 'Taylor is going to surprise you. He's wonderful as the sweet kid, but even better as the angry werewolf. The kid can act.'

Stretch Armstrong

We're going to get to see a lot of Taylor in 2012 because he has signed up to play *Stretch Armstrong* in a 3D movie of the same name.

Stretch Armstrong has been around for a long time – since 1976, in fact. He is a Hasbro toy with arms and legs that stretch and his usual opponent is his evil brother, Evil X-ray Wretch Armstrong. It's not known if Taylor will fight him or whether another archenemy is to be created.

The movie is to be produced by Brian Grazer, who is one of the best in the business. He has worked with Angelina Jolie in *The Changeling*, Michael Sheen in *Frost/Nixon* and Eminem in *8 Mile*. A cartoon version of Brian has appeared twice on *The Simpsons*, too.

Brian released a statement in June 2009, saying: '*Stretch Armstrong* is a character I have wanted to see on screen for a long time. He's an unconventional kind of superhero with a power that no one would want. It's a story about a guy stretching – if you will – the limits of what is possible to become all that he can be.'

Universal were thrilled to get Taylor onboard. Donna Langley, co-chairman of Universal Studios, said: 'In the past two years Taylor has emerged as a real star at the global box office. He brings the perfect balance of energy and athleticism to the role of an unlikely superhero with a fantastic superpower. We couldn't be more pleased that he has agreed to be our Stretch.'

The original stretch toy has blond hair so we'll have to wait and see if Taylor has to dye his hair – it would be weird seeing him without his dark locks.

Stunts

If Taylor wasn't an actor he would be a great stuntman: he may only be young, but he is at the peak of physical fitness and his martial arts skills are so advanced that he makes the most complicated stunts look easy.

The *Twilight Saga* directors have all respected Taylor's wish to do his own stunts and have allowed him to do as many as possible without risking his own safety. Because the movies were made really close together, they couldn't afford for Taylor to break a leg or an arm – it

TAYLOR ENJOYS DAREDEVIL ACTIVITIES SUCH AS GO-KARTING.

would really hold them up and might potentially cost the studio millions.

At the beginning of *New Moon* Taylor was given an evaluation to see what he could do. It was probably quite nerve-wracking for him to perform in a sports hall, knowing that his every move was being watched. Those monitoring him put him on dirt bikes as well because he would have to ride one in *New Moon* and they wanted to see how much natural ability he had. Taylor finds doing stunts loads of fun and so he was thrilled when he got the thumbs-up.

But Taylor did have help with his stunt work and he wouldn't have been able to do his stunts in the first place if it wasn't for his trainer, who helped him loads. He owes him a lot.

While promoting *New Moon*, Taylor told iesb.com: 'The physical side was really fun. Some of it was challenging – I'd never ridden a dirt bike before. Yes, I rode the dirt bike for a total of about five seconds in the film, but for those five seconds, I had to look as cool as possible, so it did require a lot of practice, safety-wise, for them to let me do it. And, like when I run up the side of Bella's house, the wires were there so that if I slipped and fell, I didn't face plant into the ground. It was definitely challenging.

That stunt was really complicated. I was using a little plug in the side of the wall to take off from and jump, so it was really complicated and it required a lot of practice.

Every single weekend, I would practise that stunt, for three hours a day. It was the last thing we filmed.'

Kristen Stewart wasn't anywhere near as comfortable as Taylor doing the bike stunts. She thought the way he handled it was incredible, as she explained to About.com: 'I'm definitely never going to be a biker. The idea of riding, I mean I'm scared of cars, so the idea of riding a motorcycle is just never going to be something that I'm into. I was towed ridiculously. I was on the back of this truck and I probably looked funny doing it. Taylor rode motorcycles really well. There's this one part that's sort of undeniably him – he rides up and skids. I left that to him. I wasn't about to do that. I don't even think that they would let me necessarily – they would have more faith in Taylor to do that.'

Anyone who watches the way Jacob climbs through Bella's bedroom window can't help but be impressed by Taylor's dedication and skill to get the scene right. It looks so smooth that you could easily be fooled into thinking it was computer-generated.

Taylor also did his own stunt work when he was twelve and filming *The Adventures of Sharkboy and Lavagirl 3-D*. Robert Rodriguez was really impressed with his martial arts skills and let him do his own choreography for the fight scenes. Taylor would show him a number of routines that he had devised and then Robert would edit his favourite bits to be in the movie.

Superheroes

Every male on the planet, man and boy, is a superhero fan and Taylor is no exception. He might love action movies, but he also enjoys watching movies about superheroes, too. Taylor has watched all the *Spider-Man* movies and thinks they're great, even though Peter Parker/Spiderman isn't his favourite superhero of all time.

As well as watching superhero movies, Taylor has also thought about what superpowers he would pick, given the opportunity to be a superhero. He says that he would want x-ray vision like Superman so he could see straight through things.

T is for...

Taylor Dooley

Taylor became really good friends with Taylor Dooley while they were filming *The Adventures of Sharkboy and Lavagirl 3-D*. It was a bit confusing on set and in the interviews they gave to promote the movie because they share the same first name.

Both Taylors have a lot in common. At the time, our favourite actor told the *Oregon Herald*: 'It's really weird – our moms have the same name, we both have younger siblings, and we live practically across the street from each other in LA. If I were to drive to her house, it would take only seconds!'

TAYLOR, SASHA PIETERSE AND TAYLOR.

Since filming wrapped, people have suggested the two Taylors might be dating but Taylor Dooley insists this isn't true, despite spending New Year's Eve 2009 with the Lautner family.

After being asked if Taylor was her boyfriend, she wrote on her official website: 'Taylor is one of my close friends. I know a lot of you ask this question because you have seen us in *so* many photos together. That is because we did so much publicity for *Shark Boy and Lavagirl* together and our families are very close, so we get to hang out a lot. So don't worry girls, he's still available and we are just friends!'

Poor Taylor is always being linked to his female friends – it must be such a pain not being able to go out for a burger or go bowling with a girl without the paparazzi following their every move and newspapers printing stories that say they are dating.

Taylor Swift

The talented singer Taylor Swift is the second female Taylor that our favourite actor has been linked with. Unlike Taylor Dooley, Taylor Swift is actually older than Taylor Lautner by three years.

Because Taylor Lautner likes to keep his private life private, he has never admitted that he might be anything

TAYLOR MET TAYLOR SWIFT ON THE SET OF *VALENTINE'S DAY*.

more than friends with Taylor Swift. During an interview with *Rolling Stone* magazine, however, the interviewer asked him if they were together and he replied, 'Possibly.' He said they 'instantly clicked' on the set of their movie *Valentine's Day* and blurted out: 'She's an amazing girl. Aside from being beautiful, she's extremely funny, charismatic and fun to be around, so we definitely got along. We're close.'

Despite the fact Taylor never admitted that he was dating the 'You Belong With Me' hitmaker, on 29 December 2009, the world's media speculated the two had been dating, but had now split up. An official statement still has to be released, so we don't know exactly what happened. For now, however, their friendship is still going strong. Alongside their publicists, they were photographed going for lunch at The Farm of Beverly Hills on 24 March 2010. No one knows for sure what is happening apart from the two Taylors themselves!

FUN FACT

If the two Taylors do end up having a long-term relationship and eventually get married, they will have the same name. Both will be called Taylor Lautner!

Teeth

Taylor might be the perfect gentleman now, but he wasn't always like that. At nursery, he wasn't always well behaved and sometimes showed other children his teeth. He admitted to one journalist: 'I was a biter at day-care. I don't remember it, but my parents tell me I'd bite other kids.'

When he was playing Sharkboy back in 2005, Taylor had to wear shark teeth over his normal ones. The fake teeth were made of rubber and he had to slip them over his own teeth whenever he was about to shoot a scene when his character got mad. When his character had a 'mini-shark frenzy' he had to put them over his bottom teeth and leave the top ones as they were.

Taylor wasn't at all impressed at having to wear the shark teeth because they were unpredictable and could even fall out as he was talking. This proved quite dangerous – he once choked on a set of fake teeth. He also thought they made him look ugly!

Luckily for Taylor, he hasn't had to wear fake teeth for any of his other movies that he has done since then. He *has* worn them in photo shoots, though: Taylor, Rob, Kellan, Jackson and Cam did a really funny photo shoot for *VMan* magazine, back in April 2009, when they posed with plastic fangs and messed around. They all looked really sexy, especially Taylor!

In early 2010, Taylor won a 'Teen Vogue Beauty Award' for having the Best Smile. He did so well because lots of celebrities have great teeth (and smiles) in Hollywood. Many of them have had to have work done to their teeth, but Taylor's own teeth are so perfect that he hasn't needed to do this. His good friend Taylor Swift also picked up a Teen Vogue Beauty Award, but hers was for Best Hair.

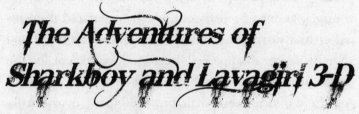

The Adventures of Sharkboy and Lavagirl 3-D

Taylor's first big role was in the kids' action and adventure movie, *The Adventures of Sharkboy and Lavagirl 3-D*. It was filmed on location in Texas, so Taylor had to move there for three months. At the time, he was only 13-years-old.

The movie was released on 10 June 2005 in the USA and a few months later, on 26 August, hit the UK cinemas. It tells the story of a young boy called Max, who gets bullied at school and is a bit of a daydreamer. During one class, he starts to dream about two superheroes, Sharkboy and Lavagirl. Later, they come to life and ask him to help them save their home world as evil Mr Electric is trying to destroy it. Only Max is able to stop him. During the movie, the three of them go on lots of different adventures to save Sharkboy and Lavagirl's home world. Really, it's the kind of movie that is suitable for all audiences!

Taylor loved playing Sharkboy because he's such an interesting character. Rather than living the life of the average schoolboy, he was actually raised by sharks! In an interview with Mark Sells from *The Reel Deal*, Taylor gushed: 'Well, first of all he's a superhero. When he was younger, about five years old, he was separated from his father in a storm. His father was a marine biologist and after his father disappeared, he was alone except for the sharks. Raised by sharks, he became very self-confident. And he winds up being half-boy, half-shark, occasionally going into these shark frenzies, where he starts biting and ripping stuff. He gets really, really crazy, and that's when you don't want to be near him. But he was fun to play because he got to do a lot of acrobatic stuff. And he gets to move like a shark and throw lots and lots of temper tantrums!'

Taylor also loved playing Sharkboy because he had worked so hard to get the part in the first place. He went up against thousands of other talented boys, but still managed to end up on top.

Taylor's first audition was on a really small scale with just a casting director. They didn't really give him much feedback at the end of the audition, just said thanks and

TAYLOR WAS CAST IN *THE ADVENTURES OF SHARKBOY AND LAVAGIRL 3-D* WHEN HE WAS 13 YEARS OLD.

bye. His second audition, a couple of weeks later, was much tougher because this time, it was in front of the director Robert Rodriguez, his son Racer Max (who came up with the idea of *Sharkboy and Lavagirl*) and the casting director. It was held in Robert Rodriguez's hotel room in Los Angeles.

Taylor must have been good because Robert Rodriguez asked if he could tape his audition. Then, when Robert asked him to show him a superhero pose, Taylor showed off his martial arts skills. His natural ability has always made him stand out from the crowd.

Taylor told eFilmCritic: 'I was there for quite some time. I was interacting with Racer Max for a while and Robert was filming tests with his video camera as well as getting several pictures. I stood on one hand, and I'm upside down and my legs are in a split position, and his son really liked that. Unfortunately, LA was just the first spot that they stopped at before auditioning throughout the rest of the country but fortunately, thousands of auditions later, they came back to me and told me I got the part.'

When Taylor and his family found out that he was going to be Sharkboy, they all went crazy and were so excited that they couldn't sleep for days. He must have been so tired when he had to attend school, while they must have been shattered, having to go to work.

Taylor might have only been 13 years old when he

took on the role of Sharkboy, but Robert Rodriguez had lots of faith in his ability to turn the idea into a real person on screen. He didn't give Taylor a character breakdown, but instead asked him to come up with his own thoughts on how Sharkboy should be and how he would relate to people. Having to create your own character breakdown would stress any actor out, but Taylor didn't mind at all – he liked the challenge.

Taylor wanted Sharkboy to be very confident and to have a jealous side to him too. He thought Sharkboy's self-confidence could stem from when he was separated from his father and his jealous side might be the result of seeing Max attract attention from Lavagirl. Taylor didn't want Sharkboy to be too serious – he wanted to play a fun character so that he could show off his martial arts skills and other talents.

In interviews, the young Taylor insisted that he was the complete opposite of Sharkboy because he isn't bursting with confidence and he doesn't get jealous. That is still true today: even when he was promoting *New Moon* and the reporters kept directing all their questions to Robert Pattinson in the press conferences, Taylor didn't seem to mind – even though he had the bigger part in the movie. He just seems to let things wash over him without getting upset.

Most kids don't have an awareness of directors and producers, they just remember their favourite actors and characters, but Taylor is different. He knew who director Robert Rodriguez was and the movies he had directed before he signed for *The Adventures of Sharkboy and Lavagirl 3-D*. As he explained to UltimateDisney.com back then: 'I was definitely familiar with the *Spy Kids* movies 'cause I loved all three of them and I watched them a lot. And my mom heard a lot of great stuff about him, so when I booked the movie and I heard I got to work with him, I was really excited. And when we got there, I saw why: because he was so much fun to work with. One: he's great to be around because he plays video games with you and he's really, really nice. And he's also a great director because we're shooting on a green screen for 90 per cent of the movie and he helped us a lot. He'd tell us, "Okay, this is over here and this is over here. This is what it looks like." Everybody loved working with Robert.'

Playing Sharkboy required a lot of preparation time because Taylor had to change his physical appearance to play the role. He would spend 45 minutes a day in hair and make-up before he could put his costume on (and this took him a good half-hour). Imagine having to do that every day before you start shooting and then having to take it all off again! It was a lot more complicated than playing Eliot Murtaugh in *Cheaper by the Dozen 2*. For that role Taylor just played an ordinary kid, so he wore T-shirts, shorts and trainers. There were no time-consuming hair and make-up sessions, either.

An audience watching *The Adventures of Sharkboy and Lavagirl 3-D* might be fooled into thinking that Taylor and the rest of the cast had a really fancy set to work on, but that wasn't the case. The vast majority of the movie was shot in front of a green screen, so Taylor only spent six days anywhere else: they shot for three days in a school and another three days in a house.

The Bernie Mac Show

When Taylor was 10 he got a small role in the sitcom, *The Bernie Mac Show*. In it, he played a character called Aaron. With three of his pals, Taylor's character decides to set off the school's fire alarm to prevent them from failing a quiz. When they get found out, they all blame each other.

Taylor really enjoyed filming his scenes. You can see the clips of him in action on YouTube; you can also see a cool behind-the-scenes video that his parents shot too. Taylor looks so cute as he hangs out with his new buddies in the snack room and tries on the school uniform he has to wear to play Aaron. He loves showing off to the camera and says that the blazer he has to wear is his favourite thing about being on the show and that his second favourite thing is the tie. Also, he 'exclusively' reveals that the tie is a clip-on.

Taylor seems so happy acting and you can tell from the video that his parents love him so much. There might be 30 or so people on set, but it's Taylor that the camera focuses on all the time. Taylor might find these videos from his childhood a little embarrassing now, but they make great mementos. When he's in his thirties, he'll be able to watch them and remember what it was like when his acting career was just starting.

The Nick & Jessica Variety Hour

In 2003, Taylor might have been the world champion in several martial arts disciplines but he still wanted to act and so he jumped at the opportunity to appear on *The Nick & Jessica Variety Hour*.

This was a one-off television show starring the singers (and at that time, married couple) Nick Lachey and Jessica Simpson. Taylor played a kid in the Mickey Mouse Club sketch – he sat next to two girls pretending to be Britney Spears and Christina Aguilera.

Sadly, the show flopped with critics saying that it was awful – they found some of the singing was off and some of the sketches weren't very funny at all. It was no reflection on Taylor, who did really well in his scene and was determined to keep on going. Even years later, he insisted Jessica was great to work with and that he would like to do another programme with her, telling Kidzworld: 'That was lots of fun: I got to meet her, she was nice.'

3-D

Taylor might only be young but he has already shot one 3-D movie. *The Adventures of Sharkboy and Lavagirl 3-D* was quite a challenge for him and the rest of the cast to film. Soon he will be working on *Stretch Armstrong*, which will also be a 3-D movie.

Taylor explained to UltimateDisney.com what it was like doing his first 3-D movie: 'It was kind of more challenging, but not too bad. Sometimes, when something is supposed to be in 3-D, like when I hold my Sharkboy Palm Pilot right in the camera so it's sticking out at the audience, you have to keep your hand really still, so it's not shaking. Or else, the audience is always shaking and they don't like that. Also, when you get really in the moment and you want to move around, you can't. You just got to stay in one place for the 3-D. So, it was kind of different, but it was okay.

'I like 3-D movies. It gets the audience more in the moment – you feel like you're actually there with them. I think it's more fun to do it 3-D.'

Most of the movie was shot in front of a green screen, which was hard-going for a few weeks while Taylor and the rest of the young cast got their heads around what they were required to do and how it would look in the film. The director Robert Rodriguez helped by sketching what each 'set' would look like finished in the movie, which allowed Taylor to visualise what his shark boat would be like. This helped him to put in a better performance and ultimately made the film a success.

Toys

In the future Taylor might end up having a whole toy-box filled with mini-versions of himself. He's had Sharkboy and Jacob Black action figures, and soon he'll have his own Stretch Armstrong toy. It must be strange being able to walk into a toyshop and seeing toys that look like you.

Taylor told *MediaBlvd* magazine: 'I've had an action figure before, with *Sharkboy and Lavagirl*, and it was weird. They had action figures at McDonald's and Target. I have a couple saved because you never know if that will happen again, but look how lucky I am!'

TAYLOR ATTENDS THE SCREENING OF *TWILIGHT: ECLIPSE* IN NEW YORK CITY.

Training

These days, most children spend their spare time playing outside with their friends or on computer games indoors, but Taylor was so busy training when he was growing up that he didn't have much free time just to relax. At school he used to train three or four times a week, but when he played for the football team, he couldn't train as much because of the matches and team training.

Now that he is playing characters who are supposed to be super-fit, Taylor has to train almost every day to make sure that he keeps his muscles and doesn't put on weight. He wants the lead in action movies, so he has to be sure to look the part otherwise casting directors won't pick him.

Twilight

Going to his first audition for *Twilight* was probably the most important thing that Taylor has ever done. If he had decided not to bother and stayed at home that day, he would have missed out on the opportunity of a lifetime. He wouldn't be winning the awards he is getting now and there's no way that the studios would cast him in big blockbusters. Quite simply, *Twilight* turned Taylor's world upside down.

TAYLOR AND HIS *TWILIGHT* CO-STARS, KRISTEN AND ROBERT.

Taylor loves playing Jacob and filming *Twilight* was a great experience – he enjoyed turning the words Stephenie Meyer wrote into actions on-screen. He knew that fans of the books would warm to the movie straight away because Catherine Hardwicke had made sure that as much as was physically possible in the film matched the book. She had to miss some sections out because it would have taken about five hours to fit in all 500-plus pages, but had included all the main scenes.

Taylor told Movies.About.com why people love *Twilight* so much:'All of the fans can relate to the characters. I mean, a lot of our fans are in high school so they can relate. The other thing is, it's a romance – the girls love the romance.

But it's not only a romance – it's an action romance. So I think the movie is for everyone. It's got romance, action, horror, it's got everything.'

Taylor knew loads of girls who were passionate about the books even before he started filming. He told Rebecca Murray from Movies.About.com: 'It's crazy. I'm in like, chemistry class in school: I look to my right and somebody's reading *New Moon*. I look over here and somebody's reading *Eclipse*. It's insane.'

U2

When Taylor was asked by the Christmas Channel which famous face of past or present he would most like to invite to Christmas lunch, he didn't pick Taylor Swift, Megan Fox or Angelina Jolie. Instead he chose Bono from *U2*.

Taylor confessed: 'I'm going to have to go with my favourite all-time band and the lead singer, Bono. I don't know – I've always wanted to meet him, it's always been a dream of mine and I haven't been able to do that yet, so that would be fun.'

A few months after he said this, Taylor was attending

Lead singer Bono of U2, Taylor's favourite band.

the same event as Bono – both helped at the Hope For Haiti Now fundraiser. It's not known if Taylor had the chance to speak to his favourite performer but he probably just got to glance at him from afar as he himself was busy answering the phones and Bono performed with the rest of U2, Rihanna and Jay-Z on a special track.

University

Taylor doesn't have any university plans at the moment – and who can blame him? His acting career is going so well that he simply doesn't have the time to attend college and spend three years getting a degree. Maybe when he's older he might decide to go back to studying, but for now he is happy making great movies. Kristen Stewart and Robert Pattinson are just the same – they have put any university plans they might have had on hold and are concentrating on their acting careers right now.

Valentine's Day

In July 2009, Taylor filmed a movie called *Valentine's Day* in the break between *New Moon* and *Eclipse*. He only had a small role, but it was a great film to get involved with – Ashton Kutcher, Anne Hathaway, Julia Roberts, Jessica Biel, Jennifer Garner and a whole host of other big names starred in it too. Even Taylor's original star crush, Jessica Alba, was in the movie but sadly he didn't get to do any scenes with her.

The movie's logline was 'Intertwining couples and singles in Los Angeles break-up and make up based on the pressures and expectations of Valentine's Day and in it,

TAYLOR ATTENDS THE
PREMIERE OF THE HIT
MOVIE, *VALENTINE'S DAY*.

Taylor plays a high-school student called Willy. His scenes centred on his own Valentine's Day with girlfriend Felicia (played by Taylor Swift).

Taylor explained to Trailer Addict: 'Willy is a normal high-school student – he's on the track team, he's the star athlete and he's got a beautiful girlfriend. Things are going well in Willy's life.

'I've only really done one comedy before and then I've been doing the *Twilight* films, and that's why I wanted to be part of this: I wanted to challenge myself to something new.'

He felt really blessed to be in a romantic comedy directed by Garry Marshall, who has directed nearly 30 movies and TV shows, including *Pretty Woman*, *Runaway Bride* and *The Princess Diaries*. Marshall knows what works and only picked the best of the best to be in *Valentine's Day*. Taylor did well not to be overlooked because it seems the director had only seen him in photos for *New Moon* before casting him.

Garry explained to *Newsweek*: '[All] I knew about Taylor Lautner, every picture I saw of him, he had his shirt off. So I said, let's do it a little different. We'll do a tank top, it'll show enough.'

Taylor did his own 'stunt' in this movie, too but instead of having to look good and agile, as when he played Jacob jumping into Bella's room, this time he needed to look awkward. He had to run around jumping over hurdles and then trip on one and land flat on his face. In the movie, this looks really painful as Taylor lands in the dirt and then jumps up; he must have ended up with loads of bruises. Both Taylor and his director were really pleased with how this went, since there were concerns that Taylor might seriously hurt himself.

Vampires

Taylor hates the whole idea of vampires and can't understand why girls like them so much. But Kristen Stewart disagrees – she can totally see why girls dig vampires. She says: 'It's because vampires are classically meant to draw you into the point where they have you in a complete submitting state to where they can kill you. So that's a little bit sexy, to completely let something take over. It's forbidden fruit; it's something you can't have, you just want more.'

Robert Pattinson is on Kristen's wavelength. He told one reporter: 'Edward is a vampire, he's not a hero like Superman – he's a vampire in love, who wants to be normal. I've never been interested in vampires, although I understand why they're so appealing to some people.'

What Taylor can't get his head around is why girls are attracted to something that's dead and freezing cold to touch. He thinks werewolves are way better and not just because he plays one; he believes vampires can't compete

PAUL WESLEY AND IAN SOMERHALDER, STARS OF THE *VAMPIRE DIARIES*.

with the super-hot temperament of the werewolf. Robert Pattinson strongly disagrees and told one journalist: 'Well, vampires don't have to go around with a pack! I don't have to walk around with my shirt off all the time, like a dork. It's like driving a fancy car: "Are you insecure about something?"'

Taylor recognises some of the Team Edward fans might be all for vampires at the moment, but he thinks they'll soon be swapping sides to hunt down the wolf pack instead. He admits that he's thrilled to have so many fans already on Team Jacob and when he sees them, he wants to run into the crowds and give them each a hug. Wow! Imagine if you were at a première with a Team Taylor T-shirt on and Taylor ran over and gave you a hug... It would be incredible!

Vancouver

Taylor is a big, big fan of Vancouver in Canada. As soon as he arrived there on the first day of *New Moon*, the people in the city made him feel at home. He loved filming *Twilight* in Oregon, but found shooting *New Moon* and *Eclipse* in Vancouver was great too.

Taylor told iesb.com: 'Canada is great. I've spent a while there; I've spent six months out of this year. The first time we were there, it was really rainy, dark and cloudy; it was snowing – that was difficult, weather-wise. But it's just one of the most beautiful cities and I'm definitely going to miss it a lot.'

He has many fond memories of the time spent with Robert, Kellan and the rest of the guys up in Vancouver. They had fun doing their scenes in the various different locations and enjoyed meeting up in the evenings to have dinner in the fantastic restaurants. Also, they managed to mingle with fans at band nights and in bars without getting hassled all the time and made some fans' wishes come true.

Vision Quest

On 19 December 2009, E! online reported that Taylor could soon be appearing in a remake of the 1985 movie, *Vision Quest*. In the first film, Matthew Modine played the lead character, Louden Swain. The story centres on Louden, a high-school wrestler, who falls in love with an older woman. The original movie was renamed *Crazy For You* when it was released in some countries because Madonna performs her song of the same name in one scene.

If E! online's sources are correct and Taylor does take on the role of Louden, then he will need to practise his wrestling moves. No doubt, Kellan Lutz and a few of the other *Twilight* guys would offer to help him. The film's director might even decide to include 'Crazy For You' again, perhaps covered by Taylor Swift or Katy Perry.

We'll just have to wait and see if Taylor's representatives release a statement about the movie because up until now there has been no official word.

W is for...

What's New, Scooby Doo?

In 2005, Taylor's voice was used in two episodes of *What's New, Scooby Doo?* He played Ned in 'A Terrifying Round with a Menacing Metallic Clown' and Dennis in 'Camp Comeoniwannascareya'.

In 'A Terrifying Round with a Menacing Metallic Clown', Ned is really annoyed when he gets a hole in one while playing crazy golf and doesn't get the free token that he's supposed to receive. He waits in the bushes with his friend until the park closes and then tries to have another go. As his golf ball shoots up the big tongue of the clown face, he cheers and his friend is relieved because she thinks he'll let them go home once he gets his token. But Ned (Taylor) is furious when he reaches for his free token only to find that it's missing again. Angrily, he hits the clown face's nose with his golf club only for the clown's tongue to wrap itself around his waist and drag him inside! His friend screams as the clown comes alive and stands up. Will Ned survive? Only if Scooby Doo comes to the rescue…

In 'Camp Comeoniwannascareya' Taylor plays a young boy called Dennis, who is on a summer camp. Shaggy and Scooby are also there, but they are working as camp counsellors. Things at Camp Kichihaha start to go wrong when a green slime monster ('The Toxic Terror') turns up. The kids and Shaggy are told that the camp was built where a toxic dump once stood, but Shaggy thinks someone else is behind The Toxic Terror. It seems that Clyde, the new owner, might have something to do with it as he wants to close Camp Kichihaha for good and set up an adults-only holiday resort instead. In a much bigger role than the previous episode, Taylor's character Dennis helps Shaggy and Scooby to get to the bottom of the mystery and together, they save the camp from closure.

Wolf Pack

When Taylor was first filming *Twilight* he was very much the odd one out. Robert Pattinson had the rest of the Cullen actors to hang around with, while Kristen Stewart had her own gang of the Team Human actors. Taylor didn't have anyone, but in *New Moon* things changed for him when he got his own wolf pack.

Chris Weitz could have picked some horrible stuck-up actors to play Paul, Sam, Jared and Embry but instead, he found four great, down-to-earth guys, who could act and had the right attitude to slip seamlessly in with the rest of the *New Moon* cast.

Twilight author Stephenie Meyer was so pleased that Chris cast Alex Meraz (Paul), Chaske Spencer (Sam), Bronson Pelletier (Jared) and Kiowa Gordon (Embry). When she met them on set for the first time she couldn't believe how much they resembled the characters they play. She liked the way they interacted with each other and joked around.

In the *Making of New Moon – Introducing the Wolf Pack* documentary, Kristen Stewart said: 'There's something about the wolves and even when they're in for, like a short scene in the day, it's such a different movie. It's like all of a sudden there's like, completely a new world that's been introduced, and it's warm and it's like, fun, and it's more frisky – they were a lot of fun, they were like a lot of energy.'

New Moon director Chris Weitz added: '[They're] a band of brothers whose job it is to protect their land.'

Taylor was also thrilled with the casting of his wolf pack. He found that having them around made things a lot more fun and he was just glad that they could be part of the *Twilight* experience. He explained to Hitfix how they managed to develop such a close bond: 'We hung out, while they were up here. We went to dinner, we went to some movies. We all get along, so I definitely think you're going to see that in the film. They're fun guys; they're easy to get along with.'

Taylor might rave about the pack, but they are just as complimentary about him. They say that if they had to pick one word to describe Taylor, they would choose 'loyal'. Alex Meraz talked about how much he has enjoyed working with Taylor to a journalist from *Vanity Fair*: 'His bigger role was coming in *New Moon*, so he was new to it too. We kind of all learned together. Taylor's an amazing person. He really knows how to even everything out for himself – the work, the play, the socializing. He's a really smart guy. I look at him as being a little man.'

Alex also revealed what they did together during the breaks between scenes: 'We showed each other exercises. Taylor would show some of his workout, I would show some of mine. We'd practice martial arts tricks… just goof off! We had a great time. That's part of what our characters were like anyway. We're supposed to be frisky, friendly – like brothers.'

If you love the wolf pack, you might want to check out the three hidden wolves in the *New Moon* movie:

- Jacob's dream-catcher birthday gift to Bella has a wolf charm attached to it.
- When Carlisle burns his first-aid cloths after attending to Bella's cuts, you can see an upside-down wolf engraving on the bowl.
- Jacob is wearing a wolf design on his T-shirt when he meets Bella in the school car park.

Working Out

Exercise is a huge part of Taylor's daily life and will be for the next few years at least. He had to learn to love hitting the gym and training in all types of weather to be able to play Jacob Black in *New Moon* and had to work out even more to continue the role in *Eclipse*. With each *Twilight* movie, Jacob is supposed to grow bigger and bigger, so by the time *Breaking Dawn* filming wraps, he'll probably have muscles twice the size that he has now.

A normal person might go to the gym once, twice or even three times a week, but for Taylor that would never be enough as he needed to drastically alter his body shape:

AT ONE POINT
TAYLOR WAS GOING
TO THE GYM NEARLY
SEVEN DAYS A WEEK
TO PREPARE HIMSELF
FOR *TWILIGHT:
NEW MOON*.

he trains five days a week, week in, week out. He even went to the gym on his birthday!

When he first started working out and eating lots of protein, he managed to put on seven pounds in two months, but by the time *New Moon* was filmed he was a good 30 pounds heavier than he's ever been. Ashley Greene couldn't believe how different Taylor looked in *New Moon*. She told People.com: 'It's insane! I was going through my phone and looking at all the pictures, and there's one from the wrap party that we did here after the first one and it's incredible. I was like, "Taylor, did you see this?" He was like, "Oh my gosh!" He gained 30 lbs. He's not a little kid anymore.'

Taylor's big fitness regime started the day after *Twilight* wrapped because he knew that he would have limited time before *New Moon* was made. The world might have been waiting for the studio, Summit, to declare whether they would be making another movie, but Taylor couldn't afford to do so. Had he waited, then he would have missed out on months of training time – he just had to trust his instincts.

When Taylor first started gaining weight (and muscle) he didn't notice but when his clothes started to feel tight, he realised that he had to buy some new ones. Instead of going to the small sizes as he usually did, Taylor found that the clothes that fitted him were on the large hangers. He managed to muscle up so much that he missed out on medium altogether! Things nearly went horribly wrong, though, when Taylor risked his health by working out too much.

He confessed to *Interview* magazine: 'I was in the gym five days a week, two hours a day. At one point, I was going seven days straight. I had put on a lot of weight, and then I started losing it drastically, so I was worried. It turned out I was overworking myself. My trainer told me that I couldn't break a sweat, because I was burning more calories than I was putting on. The hardest thing for me was the eating. At one point I had to shove as much food in my body as possible to pack on calories. My trainer wanted me to do six meals a day and not go two hours without eating. If I would cheat on eating one day, I could tell – I'd drop a few pounds.'

Robert Pattinson had a similar experience while trying to get fitter for *Twilight*. He told *EW*: 'Three weeks before shooting the producers were like, "What are you doing? You look like an alien!" Oh well, I thought it was a cool idea. I literally stopped exercising. Eating a cheeseburger after two and a half months of doing that – it tasted like ambrosia.'

Robert might have been able to stop working out, but Taylor couldn't. He just had to watch what he was doing and work out for five days a week then rest for two days a week. Often the other cast members would hit the gym with him so he was not alone and so they could watch out for each other too. During the *Twilight* promotional tour, Taylor went to the gym with Edi Gathegi in so many different cities but he had to find a new gym buddy for *Eclipse* because Edi's character (Laurent) had been killed off and so he was no longer in Vancouver. Thankfully, the wolf-pack boys became great Edi substitutes. Alex, Chaske, Bronson and Kiowa had to work out like crazy too, so they were happy to join Taylor in the gym.

In fact, the boys had to work out in the short breaks between scenes too. Their trainers wanted to be sure that they would look pumped in their scenes and so they had them doing press-ups and using free weights. If one of them had to do press-ups, then the others would get down too – they wanted to help each other and do everything as a team. Not many people would be willing to do fifty press-ups just so their mate wouldn't feel like the odd one out!

In the summer of 2009, Taylor told People.com: 'Jacob's character is continually growing throughout the series, so I got about eight weeks off before I go back again for *Eclipse* and I'm going to be hitting the gym. When we're done with the *Twilight* films, I'll definitely bulk down and just get lean again because I don't want to stay big and bulky.'

World Champion

Not only is Taylor one of the best actors on the planet, but he is also a world champion! The super-fit actor managed to attain a Black Belt in karate before he became a teenager and represented the USA in the 2000 World Karate Federation Championships.

You might have thought that Taylor would have been nervous competing in the U12 Group as he was only eight years old at the time, but he wasn't. Instead, he was like David going up against Goliath. Taylor might have looked like the underdog, but he soon showed his competitors how it was done. He won three gold medals and his parents were so proud.

In July 2003, Taylor became the World Junior Weapons Champion and a few months later, was named the World's Number 1 for his age in four different disciplines: Musical Weapons, Traditional Weapons, Black Belt Open Forms and Traditional Forms.

Taylor always seems to blush in interviews when people say he was once a world champion. He is so modest that he doesn't want to boast about how good he is. Since he started bulking up to play Jacob Black, he hasn't been able to do much martial arts training because this would result in him losing weight. Maybe in a few years' time he might take it up properly again.

Taylor's fans must have been disappointed when he wasn't picked to appear in the new *Karate Kid* movie. It would have been perfect if Taylor had been given a part alongside Jackie Chan and Jaden Smith. He would have been able to showcase all his skills and prove why he was a world champion all those years ago.

Writing

It's not just the *Twilight* films that Taylor has in common with Robert Pattinson and Kristen Stewart. All three of them are keen writers and have said that if their acting careers end, then they would like to write scripts or maybe direct a movie or two.

A few years ago, Taylor told Mark Sells from the *Oregon Herald*: 'I would love to go the acting route, but if I couldn't, I would want to be like Robert Rodriguez, a writer and director, because I do a lot of home movies with Taylor Dooley and her younger brother. We make a lot of films together and we're actually in the middle of one right now. So, we have a lot of fun doing that. And I'd really love to do that if the acting thing didn't work out.'

X is for...

XMA Performance Team

In 2003, Taylor was selected by his martial arts instructor Mike Chat to be in the XMA Performance Team with five other talented boys and girls. The XMA Performance Team performs a 'mixture of virtually all martial arts styles blended together with high-flying acrobatics and gymnastics.' Taylor, Nashandra Kissel, Adam Faldetta, Jake Strickland, Nicole Habermehl and Millissa Montoya were the original members of the XMA Performance Team, but in the last seven years another 16 boys and girls have joined the squad at one point or another. If you want to find out more about the XMA Performance Team, check out their official website: www.xmahq.com.

Taylor must have felt honoured to be selected for the team and to have the opportunity to perform at big events and shows. During his time there, they performed in the half-time show for Oklahoma Sooners Basketball Team and the Big Five Sporting Goods Show in LA.

Y is for...

Youngblood

In 2005, Taylor voiced a character called Youngblood in the cartoon series *Danny Phantom*. His character was a pirate and one of the bad guys. He did really well in this role, putting a lot of feeling into his voice, which isn't easy to do. Many big names struggle to voice cartoon characters because they can't rely on their facial expressions to do all the work.

Back then, Taylor told the *Oregon Herald*: 'I've done three episodes so far and he's a lot of fun to voice, probably because I'm a kid-bully-pirate. I'm an evil ghost and a pirate and get to say stuff like, "Aaargh!"'

Z is for...

Zac Efron

People might always link Taylor with Robert Pattinson because of their *Twilight* connection, but Taylor has also worked with Zac Efron in the past. He was one of the big stars of a show that Taylor did called *Summerland*.

The TV drama was about three kids who are raised by their aunt and her three friends when their parents die. *Summerland* was set in California and Zac played the boyfriend of Nikki, the girl in the family.

Taylor had a really small role in one episode of *Summerland* in 2003: 'To Thine Self Be True'. It was just a walk-on part, but it was still a great achievement because

TAYLOR WORKED WITH ZAC ON THE SET OF *SUMMERLAND* IN 2003.

he had to work so hard in each and every audition – hundreds of other kids were after the same roles as him.

Taylor had no idea when he was shooting his short scene on the beach that one day he would be sharing red carpets with Zac and that they would both be big movie stars with millions of fans. What a difference a few years make!